THE LAWYER'S GUIDE TO
WORKING
SMARTER
WITH
KNOWLEDGE TOOLS

Marc Lauritsen

ABA **LawPracticeManagementSection**
MARKETING • MANAGEMENT • TECHNOLOGY • FINANCE

Commitment to Quality: The Law Practice Management Section is committed to quality in our publications. Our authors are experienced practitioners in their fields. Prior to publication, the contents of all our books are rigorously reviewed by experts to ensure the highest quality product and presentation. Because we are committed to serving our readers' needs, we welcome your feedback on how we can improve future editions of this book.

With kind permission from Springer Science + Business Media: Book review of Richard Susskind, Transforming the Law, by Marc Lauritsen, 9 *Artificial Intelligence and Law* 295-303 (2001).

Cover design by Jim Colao.

Nothing contained in this book is to be considered as the rendering of legal advice for specific cases, and readers are responsible for obtaining such advice from their own legal counsel. This book and any forms and agreements herein are intended for educational and informational purposes only.

The products and services mentioned in this publication are under or may be under trademark or service mark protection. Product and service names and terms are used throughout only in an editorial fashion, to the benefit of the product manufacturer or service provider, with no intention of infringement. Use of a product or service name or term in this publication should not be regarded as affecting the validity of any trademark or service mark.

The Law Practice Management Section, American Bar Association, offers an educational program for lawyers in practice. Books and other materials are published in furtherance of that program. Authors and editors of publications may express their own legal interpretations and opinions, which are not necessarily those of either the American Bar Association or the Law Practice Management Section unless adopted pursuant to the bylaws of the Association. The opinions expressed do not reflect in any way a position of the Section or the American Bar Association.

Printed in the United States of America.

12 11 10   5 4 3 2 1

Library of Congress Cataloging-in-Publication Data

Lauritsen, Marc.
   The lawyer's guide to working smarter with knowledge tools / by Marc Lauritsen.
     p. cm.
   Includes index.
   ISBN 978-1-60442-826-1
  1. Law offices—United States—Automation. I. Title.
   KF320.A9L38 2010
   340.0285—dc22

                                      2010004059

Discounts are available for books ordered in bulk. Special consideration is given to state bars, CLE programs, and other bar-related organizations. Inquire at Book Publishing, American Bar Association, 321 N. Clark Street, Chicago, Illinois 60654.

Dedication

DEDICATED TO MY PARENTS, Ruth and Norman Lauritsen, who taught me to appreciate music, craftsmanship, and other beautiful and useful things. And to my wife, Joy Bahniuk, who sustains me with love and humor.

Contents

Contents

About the Author

Marc Lauritsen

Marc Lauritsen is a Massachusetts lawyer and educator with nearly twenty-five years of experience in knowledge-system development. After earning degrees from the Massachusetts Institute of Technology and Harvard Law School, he worked as a poverty lawyer and became director of clinical programs and a senior research associate at Harvard. He established Capstone Practice Systems in 1998 and later served as vice president for practice technology at AmeriCounsel.com, an Internet legal services company. He more recently founded Legal Systematics, Inc.

Lauritsen has lectured and published widely on the uses and implications of information technology in the legal profession. He is active in professional and scholarly communities concerned with law and technology both nationally and internationally. He is a technology correspondent for *Artificial Intelligence and Law*, cochair of the American Bar Association's eLawyering Task Force, and a Fellow of the College of Law Practice Management.

Acknowledgments

I'VE HAD THE PLEASURE of interacting with and learning from a brilliant group of colleagues, clients, and friends over my several decades of engagement with law and technology. For a first-time book author, it's deeply humbling to compile a list of such people. Here are most of them, in alphabetical order.

Ken Adams, Paul Agostinelli, Betty Allebach, Tim Allen, Bill Andersen, Wells Anderson, Stephen Armstrong, Kevin Ashley, Bob Aubin, Joe Bastista, Adam Bendell, Jon Bing, Kate Bladow, Gary Bellow, Don Berman, Danièle Bourcier, Michael Bowen, Bill Boyd, Dave Boyhan, Karl Branting, Norv Brasch, Andy Brewster, Tom Bruce, Chrissy Burns, Dan Burnstein, Hugh Calkins, Lily Casura, Henry Chace, Jeanne Charn, Simon Chester, Bob Clark, Dave Clough, Lisa Colpoys, Valerie Connell, Clark Cordner, Doug Cornelius, Fran Cutler, John DeGolyer, Richard DeMulder, Vanessa DiMauro, Brian Donnelly, Bart Earle, Russ Edelman, Jim Eidelman, Dan Evans, Philip Evans, Larry Farmer, Rich Farrell, Nick Finke, Sheila Fisher, Ron Fleischer, Scott Fletcher, Jeff Fortkamp, Ken Frank, Ron Friedmann, Michel Gahard, Hugh Gibbons, Sally Gonzalez, Tom Gordon, Richard Granat, Graham Greenleaf, Joe Hadzima, Carole Hafner, Patricia Hassett, Jim Hazard, Erik Heels, Jeff Hogue, John Hokkanen, Will Hornsby, Dan Hunter, Harry Jacobs, Blair Janis, Claudia Johnson, David Johnson, Cliff Jones, Bob Jordan, Ethan Katsh, Jim Keane, Dennis Kennedy, Duncan Kennedy, David Kiefer, Gene Koo, Mark Larson, Philip Leith, Stewart Levine, Eric Little, Innar Liv, Chet Lustgarten, Ejan Mackaay, Paul Maharg, David Maister, Michael Marget, Kingsley Martin, Peter Martin, Terry Martin, Todd Mattson, John Mayer, Viktor Mayer-Schönberger, Thorne McCarty, Jim McMillan, Rachel Medina, Brent Miller, Bruce Miller, Greg Miller, Michael Mills, Vijay Mital, Roland Monson, Marshall Morrise, Mike Moss, Darryl Mountain, Rees Morrison, John Murdock,

Peter Murray, Roberta Nannucci, Sharon Nelson, Charles Nesson, John Niemeyer, Mike Norwood, Mark O'Brien, Tom O'Connor, Bruce Olson, Peter O'Neil, Anja Oskamp, Mel Ostrow, Abdul Paliwala, Fred Parnon, Alan Paterson, Todd Pedwell, Daniel Poulin, Lonnie Powers, LaVern Pritchard, Glenn Rawdon, Edwina Rissland, Mark Robertson, Alan Rothman, Jeff Rovner, Seth Rowland, Ahti Saarenpää, Catherine Sanders Reach, Giovanni Sartor, Erich Schweighofer, Bob Seibel, Peter Seipel, Bob Serafin, Doug Simpson, Dan Smith, Alan Soudakoff, Bill Speros, Ron Staudt, Larry Stevens, Richard Susskind, Olav Torvund, Allan Tow, Don Trautman, Meg Turner, Cynthia Vaughn, George Wood, Brett Woodvine, Max Young, John Zeleznikow, Richard Zorza.

Thanks to all of you.

Thanks also to Joan Bullock for a painstaking review of my manuscript, and to Tim Johnson, Denise Constantine, and Trish Cleary of the ABA Law Practice Management Section for helping me get it into print.

Introduction

THIS BOOK INTRODUCES A class of software tools that support the distinctive work of lawyers and other legal professionals. We'll talk about how technologies like work product retrieval, document assembly, and interactive checklists help lawyers work smarter. We'll review the main technical, financial, and management issues in acquiring and using knowledge tools and touch on important future trends.

Our core focus will be on software tools for doing distinctively legal work—not just by lawyers but also by other professionals. And not just in traditional law firm settings but also including corporate, governmental, and nonprofit contexts.

Knowledge tool is not yet a common or standard term. I use it to refer to software with significant knowledge content that *does* something, that applies or processes knowledge, beyond just storing or moving it. (*Substantive technology* is a related coinage that hasn't caught on, except in the name of an international conference series.)

I've tried here to distill general concepts and principles and to put a lot of disparate ideas, practices, and technologies into a comprehensible framework. My hope is that you will find it engaging enough to read straight through. It will also serve as a useful reference when seriously embarking on a project.

Extraordinary new technologies are out there, ready to be used by legal workers, and even more are on the horizon. Computers continue to get faster, smarter, cheaper, and easier to use. This book mostly covers midrange technologies—ones that can seem advanced from some perspectives and quite elementary from others.

For the vast majority of practitioners, the vast majority of legal work still proceeds with pitifully little assistance from smart technology or other knowledge-leveraging techniques. Few lawyers are even making optimal use of software that came out a decade ago. We owe it to ourselves and to our clients to do better.

What this Book Is Not

Many books and periodicals deal with everyday computer applications in law practice on the one hand and with advanced topics like artificial intelligence and expert systems on the other. I am not aware of any that take the particular approach taken here. This book is more *conceptual* than most legal tech literature yet much more *practical* than most AI or systems analysis literature. I've tried to avoid both obscure theory and discussion of high-tech gadgetry.

This book is not a software catalog but an *idea* catalog. It does not purport to be a general guide to law office automation or a primer for the technologically clueless. The coverage here is hardly exhaustive or definitive. I offer it to the intelligent practitioner who wants general guidance on the concepts, justifications, and methods of law office knowledge systems.

We *won't* be covering the following:

+ Generic office software like word processing and e-mail
+ E-discovery (even though it seems to dominate today's legal tech world)
+ Applications for the business side of law (finance, marketing, administration).

I'm deliberately staying away from cutting-edge techie stuff—there's too little shelf life to that. We will talk mostly on the functional level, not on the technical level. My emphasis is on the aspects of legal work that can be systematized and the functional possibilities of knowledge systems— not the technical details. One beneficial side effect of this orientation, I hope, is that these chapters will not become dated too quickly.

The Organization of What Follows

This book is organized around five basic questions, punctuated by four "interludes":

Part 1: **Who?**—Who is the book intended for? Who wrote it? Who are some of the other characters one encounters in the knowledge tool world?

Part 2: **What?**—What do legal professionals know? What does it mean to "work smart"? What are knowledge tools? What are typical examples?

Part 3: **Why?**—Why should—or shouldn't—we use knowledge tools? Why do—and don't—people use them? What benefits and costs are involved? What are the motivations and inhibitions?

Part 4: **How?**—How can you find and use knowledge tools? How do you manage the people and processes involved? How should you approach project design and management, software selection, and billing strategies?

Part 5: **When?**—When might legal knowledge tools really change things? (Tomorrow) When should I start? (Today)

Most chapters conclude with a worksheet and a "Going Deeper" section that describes books and other resources readers may want to consider. An appendix reproduces reviews of some of the books mentioned, which serve as quick digests.

Here is a summary of the parts:

1. People play many different roles in the world of legal knowledge tools. Often at the same time. There are developers of tools, users of tools, sources of expertise, vendors, consultants, students, and scholars. Each brings special contributions and needs.

2. Working smart involves, among other things, knowing what you know and thinking about how you think. As you consider the possible ways in which to know more, think better, and work smarter in the modern era, you quickly discover that machines today can do much of our knowing, thinking, and working for us.

3. Getting more done with less effort naturally can yield economic and quality-of-life benefits. But changes in work practices naturally encounter resistance. You need a nuanced understanding of the many tradeoffs and competing pressures before you can responsibly choose and implement tools.

4. Increasing varieties of knowledge tools are available off the shelf and can serve your needs with modest customization. Finding them still requires more effort than it should. Custom systems can deliver compelling benefits, but they can require big investments and energetic management.

5. The impacts of legal knowledge tools are still just beginning to be felt. Sit things out, or get ahead of the curve—your choice.

PART ONE

Who

THIS BOOK IS FOR lawyers and other legal professionals who want to learn more about a powerful group of systems and techniques for practicing more effectively. These "knowledge tools" can help get everyday legal work done faster, cheaper, and better. Like almost everything else these days, they involve computers.

Before getting into the tools and techniques, let's talk a bit about you, me, and some other characters.

CHAPTER ONE

You

LEGAL KNOWLEDGE TOOLS TYPICALLY involve a cast of characters (or least roles): subject-matter experts, system developers, software vendors, and users. I've written this book for legal specialists in their roles as tool users and knowledge contributors. You are not now and may never be a technologist or an official knowledge manager. You are someone for whom knowledge systems are means to an end—tools, not work objects. But you are often the source or arbiter of the knowledge that gets embodied in these systems.

You are the primary audience for this book because this business is not fundamentally a matter of technology. The relevant *knowledge* must drive it. As a knowledgeable legal professional, you are among the people who have to make this happen. (I focus on the core professional activities of lawyers, but many of the tools and ideas discussed apply to related activities, such as marketing and business management.)

This book is aimed at active practitioners whose lives can be improved by better tools. It is a compendium of ideas and issues for those who have yet to engage this subject in any serious fashion. It assumes only a moderate degree of interest and experience in technical things. If you have already had experience in the kinds of programs and issues covered, though, you should still find new ideas and perspectives here.

My goal is to make you comfortable with the processes of choosing, getting, and using knowledge tools: what can be done, why it might make sense for you, and how it is done. I want to familiarize you with the vocabulary and issues encountered, to help you understand what you might be getting into. I encourage you to adopt an action orientation: allow your thoughts to be provoked and your will to be energized.

In that spirit, take a moment now to react to the following questions:

What's your general attitude toward technology?	
In what ways do you find technology helping you now?	
How do you feel that technology is hindering you?	
What are you most curious about as you start to read this book?	
What aspects of your work life would you most like to improve?	
What aspects do think realistically *could* be improved?	

CHAPTER TWO

Me

I'M A LAWYER WHO hasn't practiced in the conventional manner for a long time. Practice has been at least temporarily crowded out of my life by more urgent interests in systems and learning. My present vocation is largely helping other professionals to better leverage their knowledge and intelligence. Sometimes that involves building systems. Sometimes that involves training others to build and use systems. And sometimes it involves being a mentor or personal coach. I like to think of it as a kind of meta-lawyering (lawyering about lawyering.)

Let me quickly confess that I am hardly a paragon of knowledge leverage myself. A good bit of my own office work involves documents and tasks that could be systematized but have not been. This book is the result of a long, meandering, unsystematic process, one that drew upon scattered fragments of notes spread among electronic outlines, word processing drafts, e-mail messages, and boxes of paper. Yes, this evangelist of legal practice systems is woefully unsystematized in much of his own practice! But that situation does produce a certain solidarity with the typical reader. I feel your pain.

I do exemplify at least some virtues I espouse, such as leveraging prior work product. Substantial parts of this book have been repurposed from other writings. (Some call that self-plagiarism, but I prefer to think of it as writing smart.)

My first exposure to what I've come to call knowledge tools probably occurred when I was trained in Lexis research on a dedicated terminal as a summer associate at a New York City law firm in 1976. A remote main-frame computer dutifully searched millions of pages for any words I cared to designate. A later exposure happened over the shoulder of my secretary in the early 1980s. She was trying out a new-fangled "word processor" that magically composed entire pages of type by itself. Suddenly, it seemed possible that my last-minute revisions of briefs or pleadings would no longer punish the staff or consume bottles of correction fluid. But I had little notion of ever using the machine myself.

In the mid-1980s, after having migrated into academia as a law school clinical teacher and administrator, I found myself at the helm of a multi-million-dollar research project called Project Pericles. Harvard Law School, where I worked, had received grants from the Digital Equipment Corporation, the Ford Foundation, and other sources. Pericles was dedicated to studying the uses of information technology in legal services and education. It was one of the most ambitious legal technology research efforts of its day.

Pericles turned out to add another zig to my zagging career. Having system privileges on a minicomputer that sold for several times the price of a house made me feel that I had better learn to use it responsibly. We assembled a great team of specialists in artificial intelligence and computer-aided instruction. We pulled Ethernet cables through dank subtunnels and started getting e-mail.

Partnering with the law school at Brigham Young University around the Computer Aided Practice System (CAPS) launched my long involvement in document assembly technology. We built eviction defense, bankruptcy, wills, and divorce systems. I used CAPS several years later to write the MicroMax expert system, which could assess in seconds a family's eligibility for about seventy government benefit programs.

The Pericles years also brought me into contact with Chicago-Kent College of Law professor Ron Staudt, who became an important mentor and friend. And with Viktor Mayer-Schönberger, then a graduate student, later a professor at Harvard's Kennedy School of Government. He and I created the SubTech conference series, which has brought leading international law and technology scholars together every two years since 1990.

Those years also ushered in my involvement with the American Bar Association's Law Practice Management section (our document assembly interest group had 1,200 members at one point) and with its TECHSHOW, where I've done several dozen sessions.

I left Harvard in 1996, after finding that the community there had little interest in subjects I cared passionately about. It just seemed crazy that so few legal educators recognized the importance and pedagogical usefulness of legal technology. I wasn't making headway, and my consulting practice was beginning to thrive, so I moved on.

My subsequent glimpses into legal academia leave the impression that little has changed on the technology-of-law side. (There's certainly been no lack of attention to the law of technology or the technology of education.) I hope things aren't as bleak as they seem. One of these days I'd like to go back.

In the meantime, there are huge opportunities for legal education outside the academy. Some of my most satisfying engagements have been running workshops for lawyers and legal technologists, doing keynotes at conferences and retreats, and leading discussions among practitioners.

A couple years ago I interviewed several dozen partners and associates one-on-one at a major law firm about their drafting practices. It reminded me how much capacity there is for reflective deliberation about work even among the busiest lawyers. Law schools should be proactive in tapping latent demand for lifelong learning.

Capstone Practice Systems was founded to carry forward consulting, training, and system development work I'd been doing for private clients since the late 1980s. My colleagues are former practitioners like me. Our affiliate network includes lawyers, paralegals, legal secretaries, programmers, and technology executives. We have worked with nearly two hundred law firms, legal departments, publishers, banks, insurance companies, legal services programs, law school clinical programs, and government agencies.

For a one-time refugee from technology (I chose to major in music and philosophy at MIT), it's more than a little ironic that I've ending up spending most of my time as a knowledge engineer. I've got a gratifyingly diverse practice—one day I'll be working on forms for legal aid clients to secure orders of protection against domestic violence, the next on a system for the law department of a global corporation.

Legal Systematics, formed several years ago as a product-oriented sibling to Capstone, has begun operations in earnest as I write. We've released a family law system kit that accelerates custom application development for that practice area and have launched online document assembly facilities in a "software as a service" mode. Our plan is to deliver knowledge tools of all sorts for both practitioners and those who develop tools for practitioners.

CHAPTER THREE

Them

WHO ELSE ARE YOU likely to encounter as you become involved with knowledge tools? Here are some of the usual suspects.

First, of course, are people like yourself—fellow legal professionals—who have already begun using knowledge tools in a serious way. I would put myself in that category, except that my practice life was already pretty much discontinued by the time I discovered "substantive technology."

It's important to note that many, perhaps most, "techno-lawyers" are not knowledge tool users. Computers and related gadgets are wonderfully useful in all kinds of other ways. That guy at the continuing legal education (CLE) session who runs his own Web site and manages an electronic deal room for his clients' M&A transactions may not care about knowledge technology at all. That gal down the corridor who never travels without her Blackberry and knows the specs for all the latest digital cameras may not either. I am routinely discouraged by how few otherwise high-tech lawyers know or care about advanced applications that address their core professional activities.

So don't assume that your colleagues with the fanciest gadgets or most incomprehensible tech jargon will be good informants on the subjects of this book. Look rather for people who are accomplishing their daily professional work with the aid of software that almost seems to think for them. They tend to be quieter.

Then there are those who have crossed the line into system *development*. All knowledge tools involve some degree of customization, but constructing them is another matter. We're talking about a new discipline, really—one of working with lawyers and other legal experts and building technologies that contain their expertise. That goes above and beyond what "IT" folks have done traditionally. It calls upon new skills; it raises new dynamics of interaction between the departments in a legal organization. Many of these knowledge engineers are lawyers—some continuing to practice, some discontinuing, some skipping practice entirely and going straight from law school into this alternative career path. Some excellent knowledge tool developers have had no formal legal training at all.

Current legal knowledge engineers strike me as analogous to pioneers of the industrial revolution, like James Watt, who worked on primitive steam engines and somehow got and kept them working. They bring grit and determination to a business that is still quite messy.

Information technology (IT) staff have become a common feature of law offices. Whether you have your own or engage the services of an outside provider, law practice today is hard to imagine with them. Like the lawyer-techies, some of them know about knowledge tools; most don't. That can be because they lack legal training, are not invited into many substantive legal discussions, and are not called upon to implement knowledge systems. And specialized legal software may increasingly be delivered in modes that require little local IT attention. But you should try to enlist IT professionals in your knowledge tool efforts—they will bring fresh perspectives and useful know-how, while participating more meaningfully in the practice they're hired to support.

Managers have—or should have—a natural interest in the effectiveness of those they manage. Of course, as discussed in Part III, one of the perverse properties of modern billing practices is the revenue penalty they seem to impose on time efficiency. And the kind of cat-herding that goes on in most law offices may not exactly constitute "management." But law office managers increasingly need to pay attention to knowledge tools—and tool users and promoters need to pay attention to management! Whether you are the managing-partner alpha chimp in the local primate hierarchy, the leader of your practice group, a hired-hand executive director, or a lowly associate, you can't avoid the importance of good management in the effective use of knowledge technology. More on this in Part IV.

Where there is money and prospective customers, there will be vendors and consultants. Knowledge tool providers still make up only a tiny corner of the vast legal tech universe, but there are growing numbers of knowledge-rich software applications targeted specifically at law offices. There are publishers of ready-to-use form packages and calculators and suppliers of "shells" and "platforms" into or onto which you can pour your own content. There are online services that essentially provide inter-active know-how on tap. We'll talk later about how to find and assess these vendors and their wares and how to decide between buying and building.

There are likewise now consultants aplenty who specialize in helping law offices select, implement, build, and use knowledge tools. Few use that specific vocabulary, and they come in many forms. Some support special-ized practice software as part of broader work in office equipment and networks. Most emphasize a particular category, like case management or document assembly, and often focus on a particular product, like Amicus or Time Matters. By concentrating on system development and serving a variety of clients, these consultants can be a compelling alternative to in-house staffing.

A relatively new species of consultant showing up in law offices is the knowledge management (KM) specialist. These folks typically focus on people and processes, rather than technologies, and as in any profession, they range from genius to humbug. KM offers profound benefits to those who take it seriously. There are aspects of KM and KT (knowledge technol-ogy) that have little to do with each other, but it seems clear that both are best pursued as part of a unified, higher discipline.

We will see many other kinds of roles differentiated as knowledge systems proliferate over the coming decades. Some of us will act as knowledge coaches to high-performance legal professionals. Perhaps we will even talk about cognitive psychotherapy for effectiveness-challenged attorneys and periodically engage medical-legal technicians to service our bionic implants.

Interlude

Windmills and Flywheels

WHAT DO WINDMILLS AND flywheels have to do with law? To be sure, many would-be law office innovators feel that they, Man of La Mancha–like, are tilting at windmills in quixotic battles. That they are Dreaming the Impossible Dream. And we all know from personal experience how hard it can be to resist the heavy wheel of inertia that seems to turn in many law offices. Get on the wrong side of that baby and you're likely to get squashed.

But I have happier metaphors in mind. Let's think about how the principles behind these old mechanical technologies might be applied to us knowledge workers. Do they point to ways in which lawyers can work smarter? Do the benefits of working smarter outweigh the costs? How do we go about changing?

Spinning Our Wheels

A windmill is a device of ancient origin that taps the energy of the wind by means of sails mounted on a rotating shaft. It *translates* energy that is often abundantly present all around us into a form that can be harnessed for human purposes, like pumping water, cutting wood, and grinding grain. In early times, windmills were typically mounted on vertical shafts, which resulted in sails only being propelled by the wind on half of their rotation. By the mid-1700s, they spun on horizontal shafts, and the fantail was introduced to turn the sails square into the wind.

Even if we can't directly exploit the abundance of hot air that blows around law offices with little desktop windmills, there is a continuous flow of information and knowledge that *can* be harnessed. Lawyers and other legal professionals are constantly acquiring and dispensing knowledge. Without proper management, much of this knowledge flows away without performing useful work. New technologies provide ways to enable knowledge gathered for one purpose to do intellectual labor in collateral projects.

A flywheel is a heavy wheel that is attached to the shaft of a machine for the purpose of storing and releasing rotational energy. It is a classic example of a technology for *storing* energy. The flywheel was an important part of the original steam engine and the internal combustion engine. It served both to store energy delivered from the reciprocating motion of pistons and to regulate the speed of the shaft by supplying inertial energy between strokes. Modern-day flywheels, with space-age materials made to rotate at enormous speeds in vacuum chambers, can store and release enough energy to power zero-emission automobiles for long distances. These devices can be spun up to high speeds at a kind of filling station and then generate continuous electrical energy through magnetic effects, which powers the car's motors. Flywheel technology is being deployed in such varied contexts as satellites, trains, and uninterruptible power supplies.

Once again, it probably doesn't make sense to install physical flywheels in law offices to store the energy involved, say, in lawyers' repetitive lifts of telephone handsets or the banging of fists at the negotiation table. But *metaphorical* flywheels are very much in order. We can use information technology to capture intellectual energy before it dissipates; bottle it up, as it were; and redeploy that energy in later contexts when it can do some good. These knowledge flywheels can gather energy in slow times that can help meet demand in boom periods—that is, capture *potential* energy.

One practical approach to building storehouses of legal intellectual energy is to organize our know-how into so-called substantive systems. These are specialized tools for law practice that embody substantive legal knowledge and assist practitioners in such tasks as organizing facts, making legal decisions, drafting documents, and planning and tracking events. By their nature, they focus on a particular area of practice.

You'll read about some of the technologies involved in coming chapters.

Changing Economics

Until recently, the economic rationality of knowledge systems has been dubious. But things are changing.

Law practice is being buffeted with changes from a variety of directions. Corporate clients are exerting downward pressure on prices while expecting improved performance. Technology comparisons with other firms are a more common consideration in firm selection. Task-based billing has grown in acceptance.

Lawyers face new kinds of competition from nontraditional service providers. Accounting firms, consultants, and others are entering businesses previously considered safe legal turf. Temporary legal services and boutiques are changing how work is allocated. Overseas providers are beginning to radically undercut the price of legal research, writing, and due diligence. Online legal assistance sites have proliferated.

Clients themselves are starting to build in-house repositories and systems. Independent legal research services, like the Legal Research Network, have begun to prosper. Charging twice for the same research memo is becoming less feasible. And there has been a growth in public and quasi-public knowledge bases on the World Wide Web and specialized services like FindLaw.

In short, lawyers find themselves having to do more for less, in sharper competition with other providers who tend to make more active use of technology.

Land Reclamation and Virtuous Circles

Over the course of several centuries, the Dutch used windmills as a key technology in the major public works project that reclaimed millions of acres of land from the North Sea. Could it be that lawyers can use cognitive windmills to reclaim or protect territories of professional practice? Can we expect to compete with accountants and other nontraditional legal service providers if we don't modernize? How can we tap into the huge unserved market for *affordable* legal services? Isn't there an alternative to the vicious spiral toward oblivion that parts of the profession seem to be following?

Let's also reinvent the flywheel—as a machine of *virtuous* circles, where current investments deliver ongoing payoffs. Rather than just turning the crank, or having our spiritual backs broken on the lumbering wheel of the "way we've always done things," let's rev up new machinery for storing and reusing cognitive horsepower.

To do this, we need to take knowledge seriously. It should be front and center in our attention. Clients and colleagues want *knowledgeable people working smart.*

PART TWO

What

IN THIS SECTION, WE'LL cover some definitional and conceptual background. We'll review the many kind of things lawyers know and some characteristics of that knowledge. We'll talk *non*-technologically about working smart before launching into the roles technology can play. Then we'll move on to illustrative categories of knowledge tools:

- ◆ Case/matter management and related "managers"
- ◆ Work product retrieval
- ◆ Document assembly
- ◆ Interactive questionnaires
- ◆ Intelligent checklists
- ◆ Expert systems and artificial intelligence
- ◆ Online systems
- ◆ Decision support tools

CHAPTER FOUR

Working Smart

WHEN WE THINK ABOUT working smart, one of the first slogans that occurs to us is that we should avoid "reinventing the wheel." The notion of devoting energy to a task that results in something already present epitomizes working dumb. (Few firms attract customers with the sign "Wheels Reinvented Here.") Knowledge conservation thus can be said to be one of the bedrocks of smart work. But there are lots of others. In this chapter, we'll review commonsense things people can (or should) do in the workplace to work effectively. Very little of that turns out to have much to do with technology.

"Work smart, not hard" is a familiar admonition. You can buy posters with titles like "101 Ways to Work Smarter, not Harder." There are loads of books, articles, and seminars on the subject, often under the rubric of time management.

A lot of working smart is just common sense. "Measure twice, cut once." "Begin with the end in mind." "Don't be pennywise and pound foolish."

Working smart isn't efficiency for efficiency's sake. It doesn't require time-and-motion studies or modern-day efficiency experts.

Here are some basic working smart strategies that relate to professional legal work and the various forms of knowledge involved in that work. Consult the books listed at the end of this chapter for deeper coverage.

A core goal is to get desired results with the minimum of effort. Get more done with less, and avoid unnecessary motion. One aspect of this is to *reuse rather than redo*. Don't do things more than once if you don't need to.

Reuse is a form of resource optimization. You can practice knowledge conservation by getting good returns on your intellectual investments. Use the hard-won knowledge you already have.

How can you get future value out of present work? (Or, from the future's point of view, extract value from past work?)

First, *be alert to opportunities for reuse*. When starting something new, spend some time thinking about existing knowledge you can exploit or knowledge reuse opportunities you can seize. Use whatever you have that's useful, whether or not it was created with an eye toward reuse. Good search tools and methods obviously make this easier.

Second, *anticipate and facilitate reuse*. When two roughly similar ways of proceeding are presented, choose the one that leaves more reusable knowledge for posterity. Take extra time to memorialize discovered knowledge and know-how while it is still fresh. Think "What did we learn from this case? What mistakes did we make?" Leave a legacy. Try to crystallize generalizable rules. Notice regularities.

Just saving the final work product can mean the loss of lots of valuable stuff. Reference material and intermediate products are also often worth saving. Record alternative arguments and strategies that you considered but rejected, provisions you played with but dropped. Make contemporaneous notes about tools and materials you *wish* you had. ("What do I wish I saved *last* time?" "Gee, it would really have been useful if I had saved that list of all of arguments we ended up *not* using, and the reasons.") Usually the cost of recording, preserving, and retrieving knowledge is less than the cost of reacquiring it.

Third, *find work that uses existing knowledge assets*. Try to get engagements that allow you to make the best use of existing knowledge and skills.

In addition to reusing past work, you can sometimes accomplish several things with one contemporary process. Be alert to opportunities to "double dip," or to get multiple bangs for the buck. A survey of new developments in an area of law for a client may also provide raw material for a CLE presentation.

A related tactic is to *multitask*—i.e., do several tasks concurrently. While some forms of multitasking involve switches and divisions of attention that reduce overall effectiveness, it is often possible to interleave processes that require only intermittent attention.

Delegation is often mentioned as a species of working smart. Shift work to people who can do it most cost-effectively. Person-shifting is facilitated by systematizing the tasks involved. If they are especially well systematized, you may even be able to offload them to machines. (That's a lot of what we'll be covering in the rest of this book.)

Planning work is, of course, smart. Doing things in an optimal sequence, and doing them right the first time, requires some thought. It helps to think ahead. Sometimes you can't get the resources right when you need them. (A solar-powered night-light is of little use.) Plan trips and tasks to avoid retracing your steps.

Staging your work well is another key discipline. Get needed materials and tools within easy reach. If you are like most people, you find it hard to preserve detailed knowledge about, or working expertise in, more than a few relatively narrow subjects at a time. When you stray from these areas into others, ramping-up time is required. Mnemonic aids can make this less of an effort. There are lots of strategies for remembering knowledge states. They can be simple notes, outlines, diagrams, or other reminders.

"Keep your axe sharp" is a useful mantra. More broadly, invest appropriately in your production capacity. That involves people, tools, and other aspects of your work environment. It includes cultivating habits of mind that respect continuous learning and improvement. Make working smart an explicit subject of attention. Know and acknowledge your limits.

Knowledge pooling—collaborating with people who have complementary knowledge and skills—is another form of working smart. Like air, knowledge gets stale and depleted if it doesn't circulate.

Systemization is a key form of greater personal and organizational effectiveness. Good systems help you get quality work done with less effort and stress. Arguably all forms of working smart come down to being systematic.

Most of us eventually stumble onto a repertoire of methods that work for us. We develop ways to cope with knowledge management. Lots of practical techniques—like the "funnel method" in taking depositions—involve aspects of working smart. We vary both in terms of our effectiveness in knowledge management and our consciousness and concern about that effectiveness. Most established practitioners are reasonably smart about working smart already. Not all of us can be world-class knowledge athletes. What we're talking about here is gaining an edge. Getting a better "return on effort."

Working smart nowadays often involves *crafting and wielding power tools*. When and how to make intelligent use of such tools is the main focus of this book. We all have a lot to learn about how to work most effectively with them.

Take some time to identify and congratulate yourself for ways in which you already work smart. Then soberly reflect on whether even they may not be as smart as you think.

Describe three work activities you do often in as much detail as possible.	
In what ways do you feel that you currently work smart? Name at least five.	
In what respects do you think that "there's gotta be a better way"?	
What general techniques for working smart would you add to the list in this chapter?	
Imagine you had a brilliant robot (a "knowbot") at your side who would remember everything you told it and remind you of things when you wanted. What would you tell it?	

Going Deeper

Allan, David, *Getting Things Done*, New York: Penguin Books, 2001.

Covey, Stephen, *The Seven Habits of Highly Effective People*, New York: Free Press, 1989.

LeBoeuf, Michael, *Working Smart*, New York: Warner Brothers, 1979.

Maister, David, *Managing the Professional Service Firm,* New York: Free Press Paperbacks, 1997.

Rusanow, Gretta, *Knowledge Management and the Smarter Lawyer,* New York: ALM Publishing, 2003.

Senge, Peter, *The Fifth Discipline*, New York: Doubleday, 1990.

Trapani, Gina, *Upgrade Your Life: The Lifehacker Guide to Working Smarter, Faster, Better,* Indianapolis: Wiley Publishing, Inc., 2008.

CHAPTER FIVE

Well, What Do You Know?

ONE PRINCIPAL VALUE OF a law office—whether a solo practice or a multinational firm—lies in the knowledge it can marshal on behalf of its clients. While the business and social connections of a practice may also be critical to its success, it could not last long without presiding over considerable knowledge and its deployment. Knowledge is today's central intangible asset. It has replaced land as the most important factor of production. Knowledge is both an explicit commodity lawyers are paid to dispense and an essential ingredient in the documents, procedures, and advocacy they deliver.

What lawyers know and how they know it are basic issues of jurisprudence and legal pedagogy. Our plausible claims to specialized knowledge help justify our professional monopoly. We have to pass various tests and obtain other credentials that establish what we know, at least momentarily. Intelligent behavior as professionals presupposes knowledge.

This is not the place for a comprehensive exposition of what lawyers know, but a discussion of legal knowledge tools would not be complete without some observations.

There's a blurry line between know-that (what is) and know-how (what works). Know-who (who knows) and know-where (where to find out) are also critical aspects. Law schools teach a lot of what to do but not much how to do. There's very little public discussion of actual lawyering methods, especially as they relate to private activities like drafting and analysis.

Knowing what the law "is" is generally a matter of predicting what the courts or other actors will actually *do*. Knowing what "works" and doesn't— how to get things done—involves mapping actions to circumstances and goals. Such instrumental reasoning includes knowing how to sequence tasks and what arguments are likely to be persuasive to what audiences.

A lot of our knowledge is tacit, in the sense that we can't easily articulate it. (See how difficult it is to write out the letters on the second row of a computer keyboard without looking at one, for instance, even though your fingers can find them effortlessly.) It quietly informs our behavior, without being the subject of conscious attention. We access such knowledge in action rather than declaratively. Most legal knowledge in action involves cognitive tasks and processes of that nature.

I've read that expertise typically involves around twenty thousand "chunks" of knowledge, and requires about ten thousand hours of dedicated practice to acquire, and that each human being presides over about 10^{32} bits of information. The prodigious amount of knowledge required for most professions, crafts, and callings is perhaps best understood by those who've tried to codify parts of it.

Legal expertise rests on a lot of background knowledge and competencies, such as how to spell, calculate, and reason. We constantly draw on intuitive physics, folk psychology, and everyday language skills.

A refined sense of relevance is a key aspect of professional expertise. It presupposes rules, considerations, and purposes—a sense of what makes a difference. What something *means* is generally a matter of its implications for what we can or should do—what use we can make of it. Relevance or materiality instincts drive most common lawyering processes, like research, interviewing, investigation, counseling, drafting, negotiation, and advocacy.

 A lot of our knowledge is knowledge about knowledge. We often find ourselves figuring out what we need to know given what we already know. Knowing what we don't know and how to remedy our ignorance is central to practice.

Where does knowledge reside? We usually understand knowledge to exist either in human minds or in organizations of matter (ink on page, color patterns on a screen) that can (re)produce it in a mind. Nature manages to encode knowledge in things like DNA and brain cells. Humans learned to create artifacts like carvings in wood or rock, impressions in clay, and ink spots on paper. Then we moved to readable and writeable (second order) artifacts, like magnetic states and electrical charges that constitute audio and video recordings.

Most information can be expressed in purely abstract patterns—as bits, ones and zeroes, ons and offs, patterns of something and something else. And as such, it can become the subject of programs, systems, software, and code.

Knowledge can also be found encoded in patterns of group behavior and language—the concerns of cultural anthropology. Law offices will often develop idiosyncratic shared vocabularies and organizational structures that capture aspects of what they "know." The same goes for the built environment—furniture and room layout can encode ways of behavior. The environment is not neutral. Cabinet layouts, form designs, file permissions, and directory structures can act as signposts to how things work in an office.

Think of what you do as a lawyer or other legal professional and the knowledge that lies behind it. Take a moment to make at least a brief inventory.

What do you know a lot about?	
What do you know how to *do*?	
What do you know about where to find information?	
What kinds of knowledge can you imagine being effectively entrusted to machines?	

Going Deeper

Gardner, Howard, *The Mind's New Science*, Jossey-Bass: New Jersey, 2007.

Pinker, Stephen, *How the Mind Works*, W.W. Norton & Co.: New York, Reissue edition 2009.

CHAPTER SIX

Enter the Tools

Word processing, database management, spreadsheet, and communication software is now commonplace in the legal industry. Much, of course, remains to be done in taking full advantage of these powerful applications, but their value in law practice is well appreciated.

New kinds of computer programs now coming into wide use in the profession more directly support the substantive practice of law, as opposed to its clerical and administrative dimensions. These include what are variously called practice systems, substantive systems, or expert systems.

Emerging computer-based practice systems are examples of legal information technology that come closest to the core of what lawyers *do*: gather and analyze facts, make assessments of law and strategy, formulate advice and arguments, and generate documents tailored to the specific circumstances of a case. Practice systems reach well beyond earlier technologies of text processing and data management, while hinting of even more knowledge tools that lie ahead. Used creatively and responsibly, these programs have immense potential to expand and improve the delivery of legal services.

A Brief History of Knowledge Tools in Law Practice

Like most human activities, law practice involves substantial amounts of repetition and pattern. Lawyers do much less custom drafting than many people think. New matters are often handled in ways similar to old; current documents are often only modest revisions of prior ones. Techniques naturally evolve for minimizing unnecessary duplication of effort in law offices. These range from haphazardly digging out a previous file roughly analogous to a current situation, to precise searches through elaborate precedent files. Old documents get copied and cut or marked up; steps of previously successful procedures are retreaded.

In-house brief banks or precedent files, nowadays almost always implemented electronically, are one means of organizing access to prior work product. Vendors of form books, checklists, and other aids to practice contribute another level of tools and approaches.

A "systems" movement in the 1960s and 1970s spurred the development of many paper-based law practice systems. Typically constituted as loose-leaf notebooks of forms, checklists, and instructions, these systems captured an organized and efficient approach to routine transactions in which the complementary roles of lawyer, paralegal, and secretary were reflected. Many of the insights and techniques of this movement—such as the "master information list"—are echoed in present computer-based developments.

Paper media—like form books and practice guides—are passive. They don't adapt themselves to the problem at hand or the user's momentary needs and preferences. They don't produce anything. Early specialists in manual systems quickly perceived that interactive technologies becoming available on the computer offered striking new possibilities.

Spreadsheet programs like Microsoft Excel can also be used to automate aspects of legal work, particularly those involving numeric computations. Most such programs have facilities with which users can construct decision-support logic, interactive fact specification, and basic forms of document assembly. These can be useful in formulating and evaluating settlement proposals. Spreadsheets can be optimal tools for applications in government benefits, consumer law, taxation, estate planning, and related fields.

Such tools may not represent any dramatic leap in software technology, but their appropriate utilization in legal work can nonetheless make for great strides in improved services to clients.

There are many different ways to support practice with more specialized software. Most offer substantial advantages over less automated approaches. It is essential not to get paralyzed by the fear of going down the wrong path. The best way to adapt to this brave new world of substantive software is to jump in and get started. We owe it to our clients to learn how to do it right.

Things that Think

Take a moment to remind yourself about the many "smart" technologies that have crept into our world—and are largely taken for granted. Spell-checking features are present almost everywhere we find ourselves composing texts on a keyboard. We can invoke robust comparisons of documents in seconds that used to take hours of human red-lining. Online search engines make far corners of the global Web instantly accessible, often with eerie relevance to our queries. Cars and consumer electronics act in increasingly intelligent ways.

We more and more expect our environment to think for us and for our tools to be smart. Let's consider how tools can be smart in a legal way.

Going Deeper

Gershenfeld, Neil, *When Things Start to Think*, New York: Henry Holt and Company, LLC, 2000.

Ramo, Roberta, *How to Create a System for the Law Office.* Chicago: American Bar Association, 1975. (The classic manual on the systems approach in law practice, by a future ABA president.)

CHAPTER SEVEN

Three Kinds of Knowledge Tools

I FIND IT USEFUL to distinguish three kinds of knowledge tools:

- ♦ Those that store and transport knowledge
- ♦ Those that extend the human mind
- ♦ Those that perform autonomous knowledge work

This admittedly arbitrary division can be explained by giving examples of related technologies in both the material world and the information world. That is, in the world of atoms and the world of bits.

1. Storage and Transport

The Material World	The Information World
boats, trains, planes cisterns ice houses, refrigeration pickling, canning, mummification electric batteries flywheels	writing and print telephone, telegraph phonograph, photograph e-mail databases videoconferencing document management the contemporary Web intranets and extranets

In the material-world examples above, some form of matter or energy is being moved from one place or time to another, with little or no intentional change. Things are contained and preserved. In the information-world examples,[1] humanly expressed knowledge is being moved from per-

---

[1] No connection is meant to be implied between examples on the same line in the left and right columns. And of course information-world technologies always involve some material-world substrate of matter and energy.

son to person, place to place, or time to time—again, with little or no intentional change. Technology serves as a passive medium, or *conduit*, succeeding most when it changes least what it carries.

2. Extending Humans

The Material World	The Information World
hammer	word processing
saw	text retrieval
chisel	spreadsheets
plow	outliners
lever	visualization
counterweights	merge text/macros
abacus	spell and grammar check
slide rule	document-comparison tools
piano	collaboration tools
chainsaw	decision-support tools
telescope	
microscope	
power saw	
x-ray imaging	

In the material-world examples here, physical principles are exploited to multiply human muscular or sensory powers. In the information-world examples, intellectual energy is multiplied. Technology serves as *lever*, succeeding only to the extent that it amplifies or otherwise enhances its inputs. It performs its role in the "hand" of a human. Effort or information is transformed rather than transported.

3. Independent Work

The Material World	The Information World
clock	handwriting recognition
windmill	expert systems
player piano	document assembly
steam engine	rule-based calendaring
internal combustion engine	spiders and knowbots
electric motor	data mining, rule induction
industrial robots	auto categorization and summarization

In the material-world examples, matter has been arranged into a device that performs useful work, largely on its own. In the information-world examples, intellectual labor is performed semiautonomously. Technology serves as a *substitute* for human effort. It is typically set in motion by a human, and performs at that person's behest, but does not require continuous contact or supervision to accomplish useful work. Indeed, technology in this category begins to seem more of an "agent" than "tool."

Law Office Knowledge Tool Examples

Examples from the contemporary marketplace of law office technology may help clarify this scheme. Some focus on *litigation*, and some focus on *transactional* practices. These, of course, often overlap.

Type 1 Knowledge Technology (Storage/Transport)	
Litigation-practice oriented	CaseShare and LextraNet[2] are examples of services that provide online repositories of pleadings, decisions, exhibits, transcripts, and other materials involved in pending cases.
Transactional-practice oriented	Interwoven, OpenText, and Worldox supply document-management systems widely used in law offices.
Both	Online legal research databases have been with us for decades, and there are specific knowledge-management products like West KM[3] and LexisNexis Total Search[4] that also exhibit Type 2 and Type 3 features.

Type 2 Knowledge Technology (Mind Extender)	
Litigation-practice oriented	CaseMap[5] is a spreadsheet-like tool for organizing the people, issues, events, evidence, and other components involved in a case. This is discussed in Chapter 12.
Transactional-practice oriented	"Deal calculators" exist for figuring capitalizations in equity finance, and other kinds of calculators are found in real estate closings and commercial transactions.
Both	Case- and matter-management systems, discussed in Chapter 8, serve both as Type 1 storage and transport tools and as Type 2 mind extenders, by calculating dates, issuing reminders, and organizing complex sets of information for easier consumption.

---

[2] CaseShare (**www.caseshare.com**) is now known as Catalyst Repository Systems. Lextranet (**www.lextranet.com**.) is now owned by Merrill Corporation (**www.merrillcorp.com**). I apologize for not providing fuller descriptions and citations for many of the products and companies mentioned. Given the rapid change in the legal technology industry, much such information quickly becomes obsolete.

[3] **west.thomson.com/westkm**

[4] **www.lexisnexis.com/totalsearch**

[5] **www.casesoft.com**. Now owned by LexisNexis.

Type 3 Knowledge Technology (Autonomous Knowledge Work)	
Litigation-practice oriented	Attenex Patterns,[6] Valora,[7] and DolphinSearch are advanced tools for classifying and characterizing documents in the discovery process. Attenex Patterns is document-mapping software that claims at least ten times ("at 10 x") productivity improvement for electronic document discovery using natural language processing, computational linguistics, and information-visualization techniques.
Both	DealBuilder, HotDocs, and Rapidocs[8] are document-assembly engines; DealProof[9] is an advanced proof-reading tool; Recommind helps categorize and organize information.[10] Recommind's text-management systems automate tasks related to finding, organizing, and distributing text-based information—documents, e-mails, presentations, contracts, etc.

We'll talk in more detail about some of these in the following chapters.

---

[6] **www.attenex.com**

[7] **www.valoratech.com**

[8] **www.business-integrity.com**, **www.hotdocs.com**, **www.rapidocs.com**

[9] From Expert Ease Software, Inc. (**www.dealproof.com**). Now owned by West, a Thomson Reuters company.

[10] **www.recommind.com**

CHAPTER EIGHT

The Managers

LOOK THROUGH ANY LEGAL technology trade publication and you
will see dozens of products that perform one or more forms of "management." There is software for all of the following:

- Calendar management
- Case management
- Clause management
- Contract management
- Customer relationship management
- Docket management
- Document management
- Entity management
- File management
- Financial management
- Matter management
- Office management
- Personal information management
- Practice management
- Records management
- Research management
- Transcript management

And so on.

Let's say you're a lawyer or law office administrator not yet initiated in the mysteries of this broad swatch of legal technology. You long ago put in place the basic technologies of a modern law office: computers on every desk, a local area network, word processing, time and billing, and e-mail. (Notice how indoor plumbing, lights, telephones, copiers, elevators, coffee machines, and other once remarkable technologies have now become too obvious to mention? Advanced software soon will be, too.) But you realize that many aspects of your legal and administrative work could be handled more effectively with information technology, and you are beginning to feel pressure from clients, colleagues, or competitors to get with the program.

How should you try to make sense of this welter of products? Which do you need, if any? How should you decide? What are the important things to know if you are just now turning your attention to these questions?

This is a vast subject. But here are a few ideas that should be helpful in getting started.

First, be assured that your probable confusion is justified. There is no standard vocabulary in this business: key words and phrases mean quite different things across contexts. There are no neat distinctions among product categories, and there is little agreement among experts about which products or combinations make the most sense in which circumstances. There is no master plan or hidden key you can hope to discover, so be prepared to live with messiness and turbulence as you explore this territory.

Second, be excited about the opportunities. We are blessed with many excellent, mature products, and there is a lot of experience out there in their effective use. Thousands of law offices are getting great value from these products, and you probably can, too.

Third, allow plenty of time for research and analysis. Collect product literature. Surf the Web. Visit similarly situated offices that have already taken the plunge. Locate recent "shoppers guides" and other discussions of relevant products—legal tech publications are full of them. This will help you establish a frame of reference. Don't delegate this important work to a consultant or rely on a vendor to do your thinking for you. Becoming better educated and more thoughtful about the many dimensions of managing law office information is a valuable accomplishment in itself.

Fourth, think very broadly about both the benefits and costs of adopting one or more of these technologies. There are non-obvious advantages to computer-based information management, and even more non-obvious costs and risks. Vendors do a great job of highlighting features and benefits while minimizing the investments you may need to make. The investment of professional time you spend choosing, implementing, learning, and managing these "managers," for instance, will likely dwarf their out-of-pocket cost.

One thing all of these applications have in common is a focus on *structured* information—names, dates, numbers, and other data that typically can be stored in the orderly rows and columns of a relational database. They all respond to the fact that computers are much better suited than humans for processing this kind of information and that law offices can operate more efficiently and happily if such information is managed well.

Here are questions to ask in differentiating the applications:

♦ *What kind of information* is being managed? Cases, clients, files, documents, events, tasks, contacts, time, money, testimony? It is remarkable how many different species of information are involved in the most routine of legal activities. Pay attention to the objects, attributes, relationships, and processes being handled by the software in question.

♦ *To what end* is the information being managed? What functions are emphasized? Each product has its peculiar center of gravity. That may be financial accounting, event tickling, conflict checking, litigation support, work product retrieval, marketing, or any of a dozen other orientations. Document-management systems like those from Worldox, Interwoven, and OpenText excel in the generic tasks of tracking word processing documents and other application files by author, client, date, type, and other characteristics. Case-management products like Amicus Attorney, Time Matters, and Abacus Law focus on the parties, issues, tasks, and events involved in particular matters. But case managers often provide document-management functions, and some offices use document managers to handle case-management functions.

♦ *What kind of law office* is the package written for? Some products are clearly earmarked for law firms or law departments; others for both. Some are oriented toward large organizations with substantial budgets and IT staff; others for the solo practitioner or small firm. Some products are best suited for litigation practices; others for transactional work. Some are optimized for an area of practice, like corporate law, personal injury, bankruptcy, or intellectual property.

- *What is the intended scope* of the application? Individual, departmental, or organizational? Some products are truly "personal information managers" and others "enterprise systems." Your ambitions in regard to the scale of an implementation will greatly affect the possible benefits and probable costs.

- *How well does the product fit* with your current and future technology? Some vendors offer grand integrated solutions, which seem to do everything and require little interaction with external software. Others have taken pains to be sure that their more specialized products can be integrated with distinct applications, like billing and document assembly. Become familiar with the many points of cooperation—and of conflict—among applications.

Those of us who toil in the lush fields of legal technology sometimes get preoccupied with the tools of the trade. We need periodically to remind ourselves and each other that it is the underlying information and the human purposes to which it is put that make all this worthwhile. It's the knowledge, stupid! May your accumulated expertise and happy clients be with you long after today's greatest software "manages" the dustbin of history.

CHAPTER NINE

Work Product Retrieval

THROUGHOUT HISTORY, INDIVIDUAL LAWYERS and the groups into which they have combined have experimented with techniques for storing and retrieving prior work and experience. The most common way is simply by maintaining case files. Retrieval of documents and other information by case or matter builds on the independent need to maintain records of legal work. Lawyers are accustomed to looking first to a recent similar transaction when called upon to do new work. Relying largely on human memories, with assistance from external card catalogs and other indexing mechanisms, this basic approach has worked satisfactorily for most of the legal profession's existence.

Some well-organized lawyers and firms have, of course, also long maintained distinct collections of particularly noteworthy briefs, memoranda, and instruments, as well as sets of frequently used forms. These have been variously described as "precedent files," "brief banks," "form freezers," or "clause closets."

In recent decades, the economic value and strategic importance of accumulated work product has been increasingly recognized. It is not uncommon to hear lawyers talking about knowledge reuse and intellectual property management. Clients are less and less willing to pay for the redoing of research and drafting by teams of expensive associates. At the same time, most work product is being created in digital form, and technologies for accessing and using such materials are growing ever more sophisticated. One familiar way of approaching work product retrieval has been to think of having a "private Lexis database"—that is, to have one's documents online and retrievable using the kinds of search techniques lawyers have become familiar with on Lexis and Westlaw. This is now a routine technological accomplishment.

There are a variety of mature technologies for managing those intellectual assets of a law firm or law department that have been concretized in documentary form or otherwise fixed in tangible media. Any law office that has a serious determination to achieve such asset management can do so at a reasonable cost and with a good probability of success.

Information Retrieval

There are dozens of different contexts in which lawyers need to retrieve information, and in most of them they've become accustomed to doing so with computers. Retrieving primary and secondary legal sources from online services is one of the oldest and most familiar. Access to nonlegal material via services like LexisNexis and Dialog has likewise become commonplace. Vast information resources on the World Wide Web grow ever vaster. Much online material is also available locally in optical media.

Complementing the world of published and online information is the world of internally created or stored information. On the internal side, the major information sectors include structured information like matter-management and time and billing databases, collections of documents produced or received by the office in the ordinary course of legal work, and collections of documents and abstracts gathered and produced for specific cases as part of discovery, negotiation, trial, and other litigation processes. Another category includes specialized in-house research collections—for instance, of opinion letters or unpublished administrative decisions.

Structured data systems grouped under the rubric of case or matter management store such information as client and case characteristics, time and billing data, accounting transactions such as disbursements, critical upcoming events, and case activity notes. These are used for calendaring, checking conflict of interest, financial accounting, marketing, and project-management purposes. These kinds of information are typically retrieved for the purpose of reviewing what has been done or needs to be done.

"Litigation support" describes a vast array of techniques and technologies concerned with the planning and management of litigation. Core applications include structured databases of document abstracts and full-text databases of depositions, trial transcripts, and like material. The information managed in litigation support systems is characteristically evidentiary and focused on a particular case or group of cases. It is these two characteristics, rather than any major functional differences, that separate litigation support tasks, technologies, and technicians from their counterparts in work product retrieval.

Electronic mail, computer (and video) conferencing, and workflow applications are designed to support group communication and collaboration. They produce a constant flow of information, such as e-mail (and voice mail) messages, discussion comments, and process events.

The technological rafts that have emerged to deal with the legal information flood pose significant terminological and taxonomic complexities. These arise because while the abstract operations we want to perform on the various forms of information are largely the same, significant differences of functionality, semantics, user community, and vendor response have produced islands of software and methodology that overlap but have not been coordinated or integrated.

Useful Distinctions

A few distinctions are useful in making sense of the internal-information world of a law office and the technologies that have been deployed to deal with that world.

Two distinctions already suggested by the above sectors are those of *freeform vs. structured data* and *case-specific vs. generic* information. Work product retrieval characteristically deals with collections of freeform data that have been gathered from many different matters. Litigation support is generally oriented to a specific case or group of cases and covers both structured and unstructured information. Case-management applications typically focus on structured collections of data about many different matters, sometimes with links to associated documents.

Another central distinction is that of *dynamic vs. static*. Some information in a law office, such as documents in progress and case-management data on live matters, is subject to frequent, dynamic updating. Contrasted with this work in progress is precedential or archival material. Dynamic information needs to be actively managed, whereas static information mostly needs to be kept in orderly storage for potential retrieval.

The *origin* of information often makes a difference in how it is processed and conceived. Internally generated material is nowadays automatically available in electronic form; much material from the outside still comes on paper and must be scanned and OCRed or retyped. Work product is by definition of internal origin, although practical benefits incline many to include external material in work product–retrieval systems. Litigation support, on the other hand, generally involves material that is predominantly of extrinsic origin: evidentiary material from clients and opponents and pleadings, motions, and transcripts arising from litigation.

The *scope* of an information collection may be personal, departmental, organizational, or interorganizational. It is not uncommon to find work product–retrieval technology and processes at each such level. In many offices, key strategic information resides in the personal information managers of technologically adept partners and associates.

The *purpose* of information collection is a further distinguishing characteristic. In the case of work product databases, there can be major differences between systems that are designed primarily for reference and those that are designed to supply raw material and guidance for legal drafting. Litigation support systems organize and retrieve material for the sake of particular tactical purposes in a given case, such as supporting a motion for summary judgment or preparing to cross-examine an expert witness.

Document Management

Document-management systems arrived as standard components in many law offices' software environments over a decade ago. They respond to the need to track and retrieve documents created over time by groups of lawyers, paralegals, secretaries, and others. Document managers perform the functions that were previously performed by the file libraries of centralized word processing systems, and more. As tools for work product retrieval, much of their appeal is based on the fact that they become part of the everyday process of document creation and revision, and do not rely upon people affirmatively submitting and voluntarily abstracting documents.

A document-management system typically appears to the user as an enhancement or add-on to a word processing system. A database record, called a profile, is associated with each document being managed. The profile contains the name of the document, its author, creation date, type, and other information. Users encounter the software at the time documents are created, stored, searched for, and retrieved. In generic terms, document-management systems specialize in managing revisable computer files. They are not limited to conventional word processing documents but can include data files associated with other applications, like spreadsheets, database-management programs, document assemblers, imaging systems, and presentation software. The systems can be configured so that each of these kinds of files can be launched (opened) directly in their associated application from the file's profile. Several versions of a given document can be separately tracked and retrieved.

Access restrictions placed on profiles control which users on a network can read, edit, and delete documents. Security can be configured so that documents are public, private, or semiprivate by default, with authors able to override these defaults. Users who have read but not write access to a document can preview or copy it but cannot open the original document in its native application or delete it. Systems typically can track all access that has been made to a document, as well as time spent. File-naming and directory-storage tasks are handled by the document-management system.

The profiles are indexed for fast retrieval, and the full text of all or selected documents can also be indexed as a matter of installation option. Profile searches use a query-by-example method in which users fill in selected fields with values that match those of desired documents. Full-text searches use conventional Boolean logic. Field-based arguments can be combined with full-text queries. For example, you might search for documents by type of contract that were created between 1990 and 1995 and contain the phrase "act of God." Documents can also be retrieved directly by the unique numbers that are assigned to them or from a user's list of his or her most recently accessed documents.

The Human Dimension

Pragmatics

One cluster of issues often raised in the process of deciding whether and how to implement work product retrieval concerns the potential disadvantages of automation. Sometimes duplication of effort can be healthy, in that better approaches are discovered when people start from scratch. Sometimes redundancy can be productive, reinvention efficient, and forgetfulness creative.

Once the decision is made to proceed with a work product–retrieval system, there are many issues of policy and practice to settle. Should participation in the system be voluntary or required? Is all work in progress to be tracked, or only "done" (finished) documents? Should selectivity be exercised? If so, by whom? Should there be any editorializing, or just "objective" coding of documents? What about ongoing annotation by future readers and users? How long should documents be retained? Should the collection be limited to material produced in house or include noteworthy documents received from elsewhere? Should there be pointers to books, articles, and other material that is not directly online? How closely should work product retrieval be integrated with word processing, e-mail, document assembly, case management, and other applications?

Culture and Office Politics

Deploying work product–retrieval systems in an office with little tradition of systematically sharing precedent naturally stirs up deep cultural and political currents. Placing forms and precedents in a networked document-management system accessible to all has quite different implications for power relations than the traditional "forms in the bottom drawer" situation. Information is a source of money and power, and holders are reluctant to share. I've heard it said that "associates want everything in, partners want everything out." Some have suggested that experts should put "bombs"—intentional legal or tactical errors—in documents so that people won't use them without consulting, and perhaps compensating, the author.

Economics

The advance of work product–retrieval systems in law offices has both triggered and been propelled by economic changes in legal services delivery. Clients of major law firms are willing to pay high hourly rates precisely because such firms are presumed to be bastions of enormous expertise and knowledge. They expect lawyers at such firms to provide high-quality work at responsible prices because they have done similar work before or have access to institutional resources bearing on that work.

This dynamic will be intensified by several phenomena now underway. One is the growing tendency of corporate law departments to build their own repositories of documents, including documents prepared by outside counsel. Another is the growth of independent legal research services, like the Legal Research Network, which has developed a pool of thousands of practitioner and academic experts who can be deployed to perform research on a contractual basis. And once again, the World Wide Web has transformed how legal information is created and distributed. The lowering of transaction costs in finding professionals who have already done something close to what needs doing, and the caching of materials by clients, will force lawyers to be more efficient in reusing their own work product.

In the meantime, there are lots of practical issues, like how to recover the cost of developing and maintaining a document-retrieval system. See Chapter 22 for suggestions.

Legalities

Development and use of work product–retrieval systems raise many significant substantive legal issues as well.

One group of issues naturally involves questions of intellectual property. Clearly it is improper to include copyrighted material (such as images of newspaper clippings and downloads from online services) in a networked document-management system without permission from the owner or a colorable claim of fair use. But the ownership of much material is cloudy. When draft contracts or litigation documents are received from another organization, are these fair game for centralized management, distribution, and reuse? When a client commissions a major analytical memorandum, does the client or the firm own that document? Do departing associates or partners have any claim to their own work product? My impression is that the majority of law offices have not yet systematically addressed these questions.

A second group of issues involves professional ethics. When, for instance, a Chinese wall has had to be erected within a firm to prevent improper transfer of information between a group handling a particular matter and another individual or group (perhaps recently arrived from another law firm) who has been involved in an adverse position on that matter, presumably that wall needs to be enforced in the work product–retrieval system. Given a large enough firm, one might need to interpose a relational database between users and documents to keep track of potential conflicts of interest.

There is also the issue of selling the same product or service twice. Is there an obligation to disclose to Client B that a particular memo was largely based on work performed earlier for Client A? Or to inform Client A that work it paid for is being repurposed? Can or should lawyers bill for reuse of prior work product?

Other issues include the discoverability and admissibility of information from and about an office's work product–retrieval system. Client confidentiality and the work product privilege protect most such material. But where a client of a firm is suing for malpractice or other alleged improprieties, these defenses may be unavailable. By systematizing access to prior work, firms may be increasing their vulnerability to certain kinds of claims. However such tradeoffs might be resolved, it does seem incumbent on firms to develop clear policies and strategies in this area.

Future Directions

Some form of computer-based work product retrieval is now regarded as a must-have by most law offices. Commercial solutions are reasonably priced and of good quality. As these foundational technologies become widely deployed, and the corpora over which they preside continue growing, it seems natural that more advanced information-retrieval techniques will be called for.

One likely direction of demand is for greater integration across information types and functional uses. People will want systems that can access heterogeneous databases and deliver synthesized results. Perhaps this will be accomplished by intelligent software agents that can act as intermediaries between users and diverse teams of search and retrieval engines.

Another direction may be the movement from databases and texts to knowledge bases more properly: structured collections of rules, intelligent checklists, "knowledgeable documents," and other forms of know-how that conventional documents and their summaries do not typically purport to embody.

The landscape of law office automation software will undoubtedly continue to change dramatically for the indefinite future. The neighborhood boundaries loosely defined by today's categories of tools having relevance to work product retrieval will certainly shift, perhaps beyond recognition. New ways of conceiving and achieving the intelligent management of an office's tangible intellectual capital will arise. In this volatile climate, precedents for precedent retrieval will regularly be broken.

CHAPTER TEN

Document Assembly

LEGAL DOCUMENT ASSEMBLY IS an ancient technology, comparatively speaking. Advanced forms were already around when I first became fascinated with it over twenty-five years ago. It delivers extraordinary benefits. Enthusiasts have often felt cloistered on islands of innovation. Still, powerful applications have landed on desktops across the profession. Indications are that we'll be seeing lots more of them.

This chapter is a panoramic view of the landscape of legal document assembly. It may be a mile wide and an inch deep, but there's material here for newcomers and old hands alike, and I've tried to touch on most of the major themes.

Basic Concepts

Many common legal documents lend themselves to computer-aided drafting. Contracts, wills, and tax forms are good examples. A lawyer, paralegal, secretary, or do-it-yourselfer works through a series of question/answer dialogs, perhaps laced with reference material, and the system assembles a draft document. Or the user picks forms, clauses, and other components as needed from libraries of alternatives.

Sometimes such an application is obtained from a legal publisher or software vendor. (TurboTax from Intuit is a familiar consumer example.) That brings the benefits of automation with little effort and expense. Sometimes an organization develops a custom system with a document assembly "engine," using its own forms and experience. That can require a fair amount of up-front time (thinking through and handling many possible alternatives), but it can result in excellent leverage of practical legal knowledge.

Such systems capture regularities underlying the documents—what sections, paragraphs, sentences, and words go where under what circumstances. The software prompts you to make choices and specify details like names, numbers, dates, and phrases. Instead of cutting and pasting, you pick desired options or alternatives from lists. Instead of searching for phrases like "Acquirer's name" and replacing them with your client's name, you respond to questions and let the computer do the needed work. Instead of keyboarding lots of text and fussing with formats, you let the application handle all the predictable variations, boilerplate, and layout.

Terminology varies among programs. There is usually a "template" that models a particular kind of document, with "variables" and instructions placed at locations that need to change from case to case. You answer questions in a series of interview-style dialogs, the responses are stored in an "answer file," and the desired document is generated in a common format like Word, WordPerfect, RTF, or PDF.

Typically, each answer file stores all the data relevant to a single client or matter and thus can be used to generate more than one document or form (e.g., a complaint for divorce, a financial statement, and various motions in a family law system). When answers are changed, the documents can be instantly regenerated.

In addition to basic point-and-shoot clause selection and fill-in-the-blanks variable replacement, these systems can store drafting rules and practitioner know-how to guide the hand of novices and experts alike. For example, a divorce system may ask about the client's state of residence, financial situation, and children. Then, based on answers to those and follow-up questions, it will insert appropriate material in the complaint and associated motions.

In the Beginning Was the Word Processor

Document assembly systems had early echoes in the search-and-replace, macro, merge, and related features of word processing programs.

Search-and-replace functions allow users to locate all instances of a given word, phrase, or string of characters and replace them with another word, phrase, or string. A boilerplate document with placeholders like [plaintiff], [defendant], [court], and [attorney for plaintiff] can thus be tailored for a given case by replacing those phrases with specific information. These replacements are ordinarily done one at a time, by manual operation, although they can also be under the control of a macro, described next.

A *macro* is a series of recorded commands that can be played back when desired. Macros can retrieve documents, pause for user input, call other macros, and do anything a computer user can do from the keyboard.

A *merge* involves the combination of text from two files. An elementary use (the so-called mail merge) is creating a series of customized letters by inserting addresses, salutations, and other information about different people (contained in a "secondary merge file") into a boilerplate form (a "primary merge file"). Merge routines in modern word processors can prompt the user for data and launch macros.

Most word processing programs have long supported explicit programming with conditional branching—i.e., the inclusion of decision points at which alternative procedures can be followed depending on information up to that point, using IF, THEN, ELSE commands and logical operators like AND, OR, and NOT.

By chaining together macros and merges, and taking advantage of common word processing features like automatic paragraph numbering, it is possible to construct quite satisfactory systems for automatic assembly of moderately complex documents. But hard-to-maintain "spaghetti code" often results.

Specialized Programs

Specialized programs for legal document assembly emerged in the late 1970s and early 1980s. The ABF Processor (developed by James Sprowl at the American Bar Foundation) and CAPS (developed by Larry Farmer, Stan Neeleman, Marshall Morisse, and others at Brigham Young University) were two of the earliest research efforts. Commercial products like Document Modeler, WorkForm, Work Engine, DocuMentor, FlexPractice, ExperText, and Scrivener soon followed.

These applications offered many advantages over word processors, such as the following:

- ♦ Far greater ease of authoring, maintenance, and distribution
- ♦ Nicer interface for data entry and user guidance

♦ Support for graphical forms

♦ Easy reuse of data across sessions and templates

The same automation of routine text-editing processes that made word processing so pervasive was thus attainable on the more conceptual level of document assembly. If word processors can be thought of as helping you edit text with power steering, using advanced drafting tools is like being driven in a (robotically) chauffeured limousine.

Current document assembly programs use a wide spectrum of approaches and boast an impressive array of innovative features. They excel in the richness of their user interfaces and the sophistication of documentary output. See "Choosing an Engine" below for some of the choices and considerations.

Important Differences

Word Processing Documents vs. Graphical Forms
Document assembly generally encompasses both freely editable word processing documents and fixed-format, "graphical" forms, where the background is static and information can only be placed in predesignated fields.

Questioning and Advice vs. Document Generation
In most document-assembly applications, users provide information and make drafting decisions through questionnaire-like screen dialogs that are outside of a target document. There is a discrete interface in which questions can be asked and advice given. Many document-assembly tools can in fact be used to produce information-gathering modules, advisory systems, and intelligent checklists that needn't result in any traditional document at all.

Professionals vs. Self-help Users
Document-assembly technology can be and is being used both by professionals serving clients and by individuals doing work for themselves. There are also hybrid scenarios in which the client completes a computer-based questionnaire on his or her own, and the answer file goes to the legal professional for further review, revisions, and document drafting.

Users vs. Developers
Document assembly software typically involves distinct tools and interfaces for end users and developers. Many features and issues that are critical for people charged with developing applications are irrelevant to the

ultimate users, and vice versa. Some software choices offer excellent end-user interfaces but clumsy development tools, and vice versa.

Integrations

Case-, matter-, and contract-management programs generally have at least rudimentary document-assembly features built in and support integrations with external specialized applications. Being able to draw on client and matter information from such programs without having to reenter them in a document-drafting session is both a great time saver and an error reducer. Similar connections can be made with address books in Outlook or Interaction.

Document assembly is also often integrated with document-management systems. Both answer files and assembled documents can be managed, their profiles prepopulated by information gathered during the assembly session.

Online Document Assembly

The World Wide Web opened up new opportunities for organizing and delivering document-assembly applications. Any or all of the major components—the engine, templates, answers, documents, help material—can be served from a Web server, providing location independence, multiuser access, *client* access, ease of use, and other benefits. For law office staff, a big advantage of Web-based implementations is the centralization and instant updating of template collections. Access to robust document automation can be delivered without special-purpose local software having to be purchased, installed, configured, and maintained. Often just a browser is required, together with an Internet connection and a printer. For IT professionals (and budget-conscious managers), a single centralized server and staff can economically provide document-assembly capabilities to hundreds or thousands of users.

Nonetheless, there are still advantages to desktop (native Windows) modes. For example, the classical desktop version of HotDocs has these advantages over its browser-based sibling:

- ◆ A built-in library interface for choosing templates
- ◆ In-context, on-form data entry and revision
- ◆ The ability to assemble ad hoc combinations of documents

♦ Out-of-the-box database connectivity

♦ A clause library

♦ Easy local customizations of the templates

♦ Ability to function while disconnected from the Internet

Varieties and Venues

Document-assembly technology has been applied to everything from simple thank-you letters to elaborate expert systems that advise on the laws of many jurisdictions and generate document sets reaching into hundreds of pages. There is a vast range of application types. We've already talked about some of the main polarities: off the shelf vs. custom built; in house vs. client facing; textual vs. graphical; question driven vs. clause selection; desktop vs. online; document oriented vs. interview focused. The combinatorial possibilities are staggering.

There's likewise a great variety of contexts in which document assembly is used.

Small law firms and legal departments most commonly use document assembly for routine or high-volume paperwork, purchasing prewritten template sets when possible.

Larger firms and departments are more likely to develop custom in-house applications, drawing upon their own precedents and integrating with knowledge-management efforts. But practitioners in both settings are increasingly interested in sophisticated, high-end drafting applications that combine advanced models of complex documents with rich layers of annotational guidance. And firms of all sizes are experimenting with outward-facing applications aimed at clients and non-client customers.

Corporate law departments are starting to show great interest in document automation for client self-service. Cisco and Microsoft, for instance, now provide do-it-yourself sales contracts, nondisclosure agreements, and software licenses to their business users. Law departments can offload a great deal of routine work *and* delight their clients with rapid turnaround, while retaining control of transactions that vary from preapproved, "safe" terms.

In the *nonprofit legal services* world, there have long been document-assembly initiatives, on- and offline. Some legal aid organizations have developed their own systems and made them available to fellow programs. An example is Greater Boston Legal Services, whose family law and eviction defense systems have been used by other programs in Massachusetts. The California-based I-CAN! project (**www.icandocs.org**) has served interactive forms to thousands of lay users over the past several years. National Public ADO (Automated Documents Online—**www.npado.org**; being renamed LawHelp Interactive) is a related effort, funded by grants from the federal Legal Services Corporation and software donations from LexisNexis.

Courts have taken a strong interest in automated forms as a response to the deluge of self-represented litigants. Many state court systems have made their standard forms available as fillable PDFs, and several (including California, Idaho, and Utah) have mounted much more sophisticated, interactive applications. The integration of document automation and e-filing raises especially interesting possibilities. (See Marc Lauritsen & Blair Janis, "Going the Last Mile," *E-filing Report*, December 2004.)

Then there are the commercial players that target the *consumer* marketplace. There are now many fee-for-service providers of prefabricated forms aimed at self-helpers. (See, for instance, **www.uslegalforms.com**, **www.mylawyer.com**, and **www.legalzoom.com**.) Plus, there is a growing universe of non-lawyer "legal document preparers." (See, for example, **www.wethepeopleusa.com** and **www.naldp.org**.) These private-sector developments are helping to expand consumer choice—and shake up a complacent legal profession—but may pose questions of second-class quality, especially for disadvantaged citizens.

Is Document Assembly for You?

Are all the documents produced by your office perfectly unique and freeform?

If so, stop reading. Document assembly is not for you.

If at least *some* of your documents reuse preexisting texts and follow rules, this technology may well be of great value. How much if any document assembly makes sense for your office is almost purely a business question. To ridiculously oversimplify the considerations involved, here they are:

- ♦ Are there substantial aspects of your document work that would benefit from greater automation? (In my experience, the answer to this is almost always yes. But many lawyers grossly underestimate how much more effective they and their staff could be.)

♦ What would it cost to buy or build tools to achieve that automation?

♦ How much would those improvements be worth to you?

♦ Are you in a corporate or nonprofit legal department, where time saved can directly improve your bottom line? If in a law firm, can you structure your billing arrangements so that you can actually reap maximal benefit? (Systems return most value when lawyers are able and willing to revise their work processes and billing and compensation practices. Most aren't. Yet. Hint: Pure hourly billing isn't usually the best way.)

♦ Are you really prepared to exert the up-front and ongoing attention needed for success?

Choosing applications well and *maintaining effort* are the two greatest determinants of success. Document-assembly applications are fragile systems that require careful planning, good follow-through, and regular care and feeding to survive. Many law offices have had short-lived success with this technology but have been unable to sustain it. It usually requires continuity of personnel on both the substantive expert/champion front and the technical/implementation front for systems to thrive. Organizations that are not committed to maintaining that continuity should resist the temptation to start.

What a Difference DA Makes

What a difference a day makes
Twenty-four little hours
Brought the sun and the flowers
Where there used to be rain . . .

by Maria Grever and Stanley Adams
memorably recorded by Dinah Washington (1959)

Document assembly can make for a different world in the following respects:

♦ **Productivity** (efficiency)—The classic benefit of document assembly is more efficient production of work. By working smart, you generate more work product in less time, with less investment of current intellectual effort. Systems spare you from giving information more than once, giving information that is not needed, and making decisions that mechanically flow from known circumstances.

♦ **Responsiveness** (quick turnaround)—In addition to efficient use of human resources, speed of production also enables rapid turnaround—a distinct value of systematization. Being able to get things done in less elapsed time sometimes is more important than how efficiently you get them done. There can be phenomenal advantages in getting solid legal work done fast. Rapid response is often of high strategic value. Such service almost always exceeds expectations and delights the client.

♦ **Quality** (accuracy, thoroughness, error avoidance)—By capturing carefully designed and time-tested texts and methods in systems, lawyers can achieve a higher quality of work product—both in terms of legal correctness and strategic optimality. Templates assist in producing work that's free of error, valid, and complete. They can help make sure that everything is done that needs to be done and that all of the important issues have been dealt with. Plus, they minimize unwanted metadata and other residue from carelessly reused work product.

♦ **Consistency**—You can imagine a practice where everyone does work of high quality and accuracy but with little consistency in content or style. There is often independent value in being consistent, for the sake of efficiency and for client expectations. Document assembly helps maintain standards of consistency.

♦ **Less dependency on individual experts**—People can't be in two places at once, don't work twenty-four hours a day (for long), and aren't here forever. Experts may retire, win the lottery, get hit by a truck, or move to another firm. Systems can capture aspects of expertise and make it available independently of the person. Even better, they can consolidate *multiple* sources of expertise. Group know-how should be leveraged for group use.

♦ **Job satisfaction and enrichment**—Life in the law is more satisfying when we are productive, do work of high quality, are spared mechanical tedium, and spend a high percentage of time in tasks requiring human judgment and creativity.

♦ **Training and continuing education**—Systems can be used to train associates and others who are not specialists in an area. A well-designed system can serve as a kind of orthodontia or scaffolding, providing a well-guided way through the handling of a matter. A way that a novice in an area will find comforting and instructive. Users come out of the process knowing more.

♦ **Marketing and recruitment advantages**—Clients increasingly expect to see modern technologies in place at their lawyers' offices. They may use tools that apply knowledge more efficiently themselves. If you showcase some of the things you're doing, you've got a marketing advantage. Technological prowess in areas that go to the core professional activity of a firm can be a powerful source of market differentiation. On the associate recruitment front, many law students coming into firms are looking for creative, intelligent technologies in addition to the standard-issue information systems. The same is true for colleagues coming in laterally and for legal assistants, managers, and information systems personnel.

♦ **Practice improvement**—The mere activity of trying to automate practice can improve it, by forcing people to think about what they're doing. (Why is it that we always use this paragraph in this document? Why does our certificate of authority require these signatures? Why does this particular bond or this will or trust have this section?) Systemization prompts reexamination of how matters are handled, which can disclose inconsistencies or errors that have gone unnoticed in prior manual approaches and trigger novel techniques. Systematic viewpoints can make for insightful, holistic perspectives that enrich the quality of your practice.

Interactive Questionnaires and Checklists

One common feature of modern document-assembly applications is the use of a separate "interview" that gathers information about the document being prepared, adjusting itself as questions are answered. It turns out that these interactive questionnaires can be quite useful in their own right, disconnected from any documentary payload. Slightly reconfigured, they can also serve as "intelligent checklists" that morph as you interact with them.

Client-facing applications of such questionnaires provide a great way to enhance service delivery. Routine information can be gathered and delivered at the client's convenience without concurrent lawyer involvement and then later used to enrich face-to-face conversations and even drive document production.

Coming Attractions

We're at the point where almost every imaginable document-assembly feature has been engineered by someone, and where the leading products easily cover all the essentials. The technology is way ahead of what most users are doing with it. Yet there are major dimensions of evolution ahead. Two stand out for me:

♦ Support for automated documents that can reassemble themselves (e.g., based on changed-deal characteristics) after a user has edited them (e.g., to reflect negotiated-language adjustments). Right now, most engines are optimized to produce first drafts. The output document retains none of the template's intelligence. The wish is for that intelligence to survive and be invoke-able *throughout the life of a transaction*. I've started to refer to this as "longitudinality."

♦ More seamless integration of assembly engines and word processors. So that, for instance, you can work *in* Microsoft Word as you make choices and enter information, and move easily between hand editing and auto-processing. The document itself communicates the variations it is designed to accommodate.

Several past engines, notably thinkDocs and SmartWords, came close to both of these. D3 from Microsystems is one of the first new products to tackle them. Comparable plans by other vendors exist as well.

Sooner or Later

Document assembly offers fabulous benefits. Whether you enjoy them is up to you.

If you've never used much document automation in your work, take time to consider how it might help. Be prepared to be surprised. Be even more prepared to adjust how you do business.

If you're already enjoying the fruits of document assembly, consider how it might further improve your work life. Might upgrading to the latest version of your software make things even easier? Are there other parts of your practice that need attention?

Keep in mind that we're beyond these applications simply operating as power tools in the hands of skilled professionals. Increasingly, they are being used directly by consumers. People have long done their own wills and taxes with off-the-shelf packages. Now large international law firms sell subscriptions to online expert systems that deliver sophisticated legal analysis without direct human involvement. Corporate law departments equip field personnel with do-it-yourself contract assemblers. Courts and legal aid programs provide intelligent forms for unrepresented litigants. And lawyer-less entities vend interactive documents and automated legal assistance over the Web.

We lawyers dodged a bullet when the accounting firms fell on bad times. Before Enron etc., they were closing in on large chunks of work traditionally performed by law firms. With access to external capital and entrepreneurial spirit, the accountants threatened real disruption. Nowadays, though, we have the above do-it-yourself developments and the off-shoring of work to India to worry about.

Document automation has steadily gained traction in law offices. My sense is that we are entering a period of faster growth. The signs are good: vigorous competition among strong vendors of excellent products, a large community of qualified consultants, rising expectations from clients, aggressive new competitors to the profession, and huge latent opportunities for process improvement in legal work.

Before you place too much stock in my optimism, however, consider this excerpt from a paper I wrote for the 1992 ABA TECHSHOW (titled "Document Assembly 500 Years After Columbus"):

> At least in terms of quality and diversity of products, the legal document assembly industry is thriving. By most accounts, healthy growth in the use of these products is occurring in all sectors of the profession, and the corps of trained and experienced practice system builders is larger than ever. The arts of designing and using system building tools have both seen major advances. We've come a long way since the "early days."

Here we are many years later, and it still feels early to me. But it may be later than we think.

Going Deeper
Readings
Lauritsen, Marc. "Knowing Documents," in *Proceedings of the Fourth International Conference on Artificial Intelligence and Law*, 184–191. Amsterdam: Association for Computing Machinery, 1993.

Soudakoff, Alan, and Marc Lauritsen. "Unlocking the Power of Document Assembly," *Law Office Computing,* 70–77, June/July 1999. For an updated version, see **www.capstonepractice.com/keys.pdf**.

Sprowl, James. "Automating the Legal Reasoning Process: A Computer That Uses Regulations and Statutes to Draft Legal Documents" *American Bar Foundation Research Journal.* Vo1. 1, 1979: 1. (A seminal article on document assembly in law.)

Actions

Download a free trial copy of one of today's commercial document-assembly products.

CHAPTER ELEVEN

Artificial Intelligence

Nature and Artifice

Very little in a contemporary law office—other than the people and potted plants—is natural. Those who spend time working in such a place are surrounded by artifacts of human ingenuity. The environment they inhabit is almost entirely "built." It consists of desks, chairs, tables, books, telephones, pads, pencils, paper clips, staplers, copy machines, tiled floors, plastered walls, glass doors, synthetic rugs, filing cabinets . . .

Many of these objects and instruments are so old and familiar that they feel natural. They mix with thousands of other unnatural forms we take for granted and intuitively weave into our everyday work lives. Over the last several decades, computers and related information devices have taken up residence in this landscape, gradually fading into the background.

The predominant artificiality of the legal workplace—or any office, for that matter—has been true for centuries. Lawyers in Elizabethan England may have contented themselves with rougher furniture—and clumsier forms of pen, ink, paper, and case books—but they occupied an already unnatural information system instantly recognizable by twenty-first-century lawyers.

Law itself has always been highly "artifactual," like human language and its other cultural outgrowths. Such things occupy a midpoint between the born and the made, between the naturally evolved and the humanly contrived. Law is a societal technology, one grand hybrid of artifice and evolution. It's not coincidental that law, genetics, and software each involve "code" as a core instrument.

We tend to think of legal technology as coextensive with modern information and communications technology, even though technology goes back to earliest days of law and reaches into its innermost core. (Something very similar is true of music—its electronic dimensions barely go back a century, but sophisticated technology has been involved in musical instruments since at least the Renaissance.) Nonetheless, recent legal technology certainly is dominated by computing and telecommunications.

Our era is witnessing especially rapid change in the balance between the amount of working knowledge that is encoded in the human mind and that which is encoded in artificial devices. The rise of nonbiological intelligence is likely to be the defining feature of the twenty-first century. Maybe even in the legal sector.

We're already accustomed to artificial light, artificial sweeteners, synthetic telephone receptionists, plastic ferns, and fake Louis Vuitton handbags. Increasingly, we're surprised when things are natural. So what's the big deal about artificial intelligence? Are we just starting to feel that our intellectual uniqueness is threatened?

This chapter aims to supply an informal, practical view of AI's role in the contemporary real-world law office technology scene. My goal is to provide a framework within which you can place some of the many interesting ideas, facts, and opportunities.

Defining AI

When asked to define artificial intelligence for nonspecialists, I tend to use the following definition:

> AI is the study of what we know, how we think, and how machines can be made to do some of our knowing and thinking for us.

I point out that there is no precise definition universally agreed upon but that AI applications typically involve the following:

- ◆ Advanced programming techniques
- ◆ Explicit knowledge representation

Another point often made, with both humor and seriousness, is that AI is "whatever computers can't do yet." Once programmers figure out how to accomplish a hitherto mysterious cognitive task, like optical character recognition, the task seems to lose its allure. To use an American football analogy, it's as if every time a team gets a first down, the referees move the goal posts farther away.

Ironically, AI work seems driven by its own progress, resulting in a kind of arms race between people and machines. For instance, Web sites need to use increasingly sophisticated techniques ("CAPTCHAs") to prevent bulk submission of HTML forms (e.g., by those creating e-mail accounts from which to unleash spam). They sometimes present a difficult-to-read image that needs to be transcribed into characters and numbers, maybe with randomly varying rules like "only enter the green numbers," the upper-case letters, or the odd numbers, in the hope that only humans can still handle such tasks effectively.

What Does It Mean to Be "Smart"?

One challenge in talking about AI arises from our uncertainty about what constitutes intelligence. What does it mean to be "smart"? Doing lots of dumb stuff fast? Is it sometimes (always?) just the cumulative effect of lots of unintelligent little parts?

In what different ways can intelligence be achieved? Rich behavior (sensory-motor activity accompanied by emotional experience) predated genuine intelligence in our evolution; why should we expect intelligence from things that exhibit no rich behavior? Or is intelligence more like flying—which airplanes turned out to accomplish through totally different histories and means than insects and birds?

AI can be like an exquisite glass flower—just as we are amazed when an artist creates something so true to nature, we have a sense of awe when machines exhibit something so seemingly unique to humans.

Useful Distinctions

Some distinctions can usefully be made.

First is the perennial legal/nonlegal distinction, which is hardly a bright line. While I think we should fairly include as "legal technology" all kinds of applications used by anybody, anywhere, to accomplish legal work, this chapter focuses on lawyers and other professionals rather than lay self-helpers. And attention is mostly on settings describable as law offices—whether in private firm, corporate, not-for-profit, or governmental settings—where people are doing legal work as part of their jobs, rather than other contexts in which law-related activities are occasionally undertaken.

Second is the important difference between the potentially useful and the actually used (delivered, successfully deployed). There are many places in law where smart applications *could* be useful but aren't now, or may never be, for reasons extrinsic to their innate utility.

And third is the distinction between engines, or "shells," and application-specific content. Some tools come with intelligence or knowledge, while others are designed to be filled by someone. Typically there is knowledge and intelligence—law specific or otherwise—embedded at both levels.

AI in Law

As a self-appointed ambassador between the largely disjoint worlds of AI research and applied technology, I've come to define applications with certain characteristics as the Holy Grail:

1. Those that seem undeniably intelligent
2. Those that involve nontrivial AI techniques
3. Those that embody distinctively legal knowledge
4. Those that are in actual, regular, non-experimental use
5. Those that are interesting for a general audience—or, better yet, make people go "Wow!"

Needless to say, this quest continues. Not long ago, two seasoned observers began an article with an alarming statement:

> As long-time enthusiasts for the great potential of artificial intelligence techniques to transform the practice of law, we are frustrated not to be able to cite *any* fully unqualified examples of "true AI" that have been successfully deployed in the "real world" of law practice. There is as yet no obvious poster child for the field. (Oskamp and Lauritsen, *AI in Law Practice? So Far, Not Much.* Artificial Intelligence and Law, Vol. 10, Num. 4, December 2002, p. 227; emphasis added)

Why and how that can be is discussed in the next section. But first, let's review what practical applications there *have* been.

Legal Uses of Nonlegal AI

To the extent that AI-related applications are present in the law office, they are mostly "nonlegal" in nature. By that I mean that they involve techniques and knowledge content that are not distinctive to legal work.

General AI topics include the following:

♦ Logic programming
♦ Rule-based expert systems

- Robotics
- Speech recognition
- Natural language understanding
- Artificial vision
- Neural networks
- Machine learning
- Planning
- Fuzzy logic

Some of these generic categories play out in legal contexts (there are not many lawyer robots, yet—except for the carbon-based ones), such as the following:

- Optical character recognition
- Natural language interfaces to online research databases
- Speech recognition
- Handwriting recognition, as seen in pen-based computing on the new generation of tablet PCs
- Language translation
- Automatic categorization
- Expertise profiling
- E-discovery products mentioned above (e.g., Attenex, Valora)

There is in fact quite a bit of unlabeled AI at work in the legal sector.

West Publishing's WIN (West Is Natural) natural language search tool, and comparable offerings from LexisNexis, have put AI-related technologies in the hands of average lawyers. Two products from these publishers are illustrative:

- "More Like This Headnote" is a feature that helps LexisNexis users seek analogous cases by converting headnotes into natural language queries. The system is specifically adapted to handle long queries and contains selected elements of term normalization that extend the breadth of the search beyond the surface structure of the headnote's text. Target results are identified through ranking procedures that help select among competing portions of text to return optimum results in a format that can be easily reviewed by the researcher. A customized digest of matching headnotes (or best paragraphs, or both) is compiled and displayed in real time.

♦ West introduced a document-classification technology, called CaRE (for Classification and Routing Engine), both as an editorial aide and as an aide to online searching. It can be used to supplement analytical materials, West's knowledge-management suite (West KM), and Westlaw's document-recommendation service, Results-Plus. CaRE involves multiple voting algorithms, several rounds of machine learning, and training against West's formidable corpus of a century of legal materials, already marked up against a category space consisting of several hundred thousand keynotes.

Legal Uses of Legal AI

AI topics with more specialized relevance to the legal world include the following:

♦ Conceptual retrieval
♦ Legal expert systems
♦ Argumentation
♦ Deontic logic
♦ Case-based reasoning
♦ Intelligent tutoring
♦ Document modeling
♦ Ontologies

These all involve activities seen as among the core professional tasks of lawyers and belong to the second and third knowledge technology categories laid out above.

Commercial law-oriented applications related to these AI topics include the following:

♦ Inferencing systems and rule engines—e.g., Jnana,[1] SmartRules
♦ Practice system engines and associated products—e.g., CAPS, Lawgic, SmartWords, JURICAS
♦ Document assembly—e.g., HotDocs, Exari, Rapidocs, DealBuilder
♦ "Document disassembly" tools for breaking texts into clauses or other meaningful chunks, for purposes of analysis or retrieval—see, for instance, Qshift by Ixio[2]

---

[1] **www.jnana.com**
[2] **www.ixio.com**

♦ Markup tools for turning document models into automated drafting systems—this is an approach taken, for instance, in connection with DealBuilder by Business Integrity[3]

Most of the above can fairly be regarded as knowledge-based, "smart" software.

Several large international law firms deployed self-help, Web-based applications for their clients early in this decade. These include London-based Linklaters, with its Blue Flag system for derivative transactions,[4] New York-based Davis Polk & Wardwell's Global Collateral Project, Blake Dawson Waldron (Sydney), with its Virtual Lawyer, and Clifford Chance's NextLaw. Wilson Sonsini announced a free online term sheet generator in 2009.

Significant AI-based systems, not surveyed here, have been deployed in government social security and welfare contexts in Australia, Europe, and the United States.

Consumer-oriented systems also deserve mention. Tax-preparation software, such as TurboTax, is very popular in the United States, as are estate planning and contract drafting programs. Quicken Family Lawyer, by Parsons Technology, and WillMaker, by Nolo Press, are two examples, and an online expert system for the formation of Australian companies is commercially available (**www.incorporator.com.au**).

Obstacles and Opportunities

AI as a discipline is over fifty years old, and, depending on how you count, legal AI is at about thirty years old. Why do we have so few applications to show for all the work that has been done? Are there really so few? What cultural and economic dynamics have held back adoption? What trends are afoot? What developments can be predicted? Here are some reflections.

Theory and Practice
The world of AI research is characterized by the following traits:

♦ Very rich literature

♦ Long traditions

---

[3] **www.business-integrity.com**
[4] **http://linklaters.com**

- Many international centers of research and academic inquiry
- Good journals and conferences

The world of applied AI, on the other hand, at least in law, seems to involve the following:

- Scattered pockets of activity
- Occasional commercial outbursts
- Little coordination or cross-fertilization with the research world

The results of AI research and development are often highly useful but so far little used. Many experimental applications of AI to legal practice have shown promise, but they rarely mature into full-scale deployment. There is very little "industrial" research and development in the legal sector. And few institutions of any kind—commercial or academic—are dedicated to practical applications.

There are presumably AI-related tools at work in law firms and departments that are kept out of public view for reasons of competitive advantage. And there are quite a few examples of products getting ahead of the market. High-end document-assembly systems like CAPS and WorkForm, for instance, boasted features in the early 1990s that still aren't matched by applications with present commercial viability.

The Legal Industry

The legal industry, estimated at over $150 billion per year in the United States alone, is a surprisingly fragmented, undercapitalized, and inefficient sector. Law firms cannot ethically accept capital investments from non-lawyers in most countries. Work is still predominantly charged for by the hour, resulting in serious disincentives for labor-saving technologies.

Law firms and legal departments have made big investments in information technology and continue to incur large IT operating expenses. But for all the money that has been and is being spent on legal IT, relatively little has been addressed to systemizing core professional tasks, which may eventually yield the greatest return on investment. There is still deep cultural, psychological, and structural resistance to investing in that kind of systemization.

Some dynamics of the current legal industry nonetheless seem to be preparing the way for greater receptivity to AI-like applications:

- Many firms continue to grow in size, often through consolidation, requiring better systems for effective operation.

- Sophisticated clients are paying more attention to the aggressive use of technology.

- The Web has brought advanced tools, such as online advice and documentation systems, closer to clients than ever before.

- The gradual adoption of flat fees and other forms of value billing is improving price transparency and heating up the demand for improved productivity.

- Some firms are billing clients for use of knowledge systems. We are beginning to see innovations such as system developers receiving billable hour credit for useful work performed by their creations in the hands of other practitioners.

- There is a high level of lawyer dissatisfaction and mobility, and the software environment is increasingly a factor in work satisfaction.

- Many firms face a staffing crunch for good non-lawyer personnel. There are high turnover rates for IT and knowledge-management staff. Legal knowledge system specialists do not generally find law firms congenial places in which to make a career. At the same time, there is a surplus of talent looking to do legal knowledge engineering. New kinds of organizations may emerge at which advanced applications for use in law practice can be profitably developed, in turn making them easier and less expensive for firms to adopt.

- There is an increasing knowledge intensity in legal work. Both the amount of relevant information needing to be processed and the velocity of change needing to be accommodated are increasing.

- Both established and emerging economies are headed in the direction of more legal work needing to be done. If our optimistic expectations of new democracies, committed to the rule of law, are justified, intelligent technologies could be critical to their success. Globalization itself is a force that tends, at least in the short term, toward increasing quantity and complexity of legal work.

Signs of Change

People who claim that we've progressed little from the days of WordPerfect 5.1 and MS-DOS are largely correct, in terms of how core legal work is done. We now have multitasking and graphical user interfaces, sure. The Internet is ubiquitous, and e-mail has become the centerpiece of many professional lives. Most offices have fancy document-management systems and sophisticated litigation support tools. Some have portals and other knowledge-sharing technologies. But apart from the "unlabeled," non-law-specific applications outlined above, and the few law-specific examples, AI remains little in evidence.

There is, however, a growing use of lower-level, mass-market knowledge-encoding tools like document-assembly engines. Vendors now are less hesitant to trumpet AI themes. At a recent major legal technology conference, several sessions on artificial intelligence drew a gratifyingly substantial audience. Together with the general dynamics just reviewed, things seem to be picking up. I don't see a tipping point just around the corner, but my optimistic sense is that legal AI is on an upswing.

Room for Improvement

Much current legal work is embarrassingly, absurdly wasteful. AI-related technology offers great promise to improve that situation. But we haven't yet seen much interaction between inventors and scholars on the one side and business people and users on the other.

What percentage of legal work that *could* be cost-effectively performed by intelligent software *is* so being performed? My instinct is that the answer is a very small percentage, certainly in the single digits. There is a vast potential market for good-quality, reasonably priced knowledge systems and services.

Lawyers need to consider where knowledge tools make business sense. Only in value billing? How will practice be different in a world of "things that think"?

Knowledge technologists and researchers should consider how the fruits of their labor can be ripened by enlisting practitioner input.

Law is important, maybe critical, for the future of global justice and prosperity. Knowledge technology, appropriately managed, is important, maybe critical, for the future of law. Those of us who know and care about both things need to exert disciplined and energetic effort if we expect positive change.

Going Deeper
Readings

Berman, Donald, and Carole Hafner, "The Potential of Artificial Intelligence to Help Solve the Crisis in Our Legal System," *Communications of the ACM*, 928, August 1989.

Hokkanen, John, and Marc Lauritsen, "Knowledge Tools for Legal Knowledge Tool Makers," *Artificial Intelligence and Law.* Vol. 10, No. 4, 295–302, 2003.

Kurzweil, Ray, *The Age of Spiritual Machines: When Computers Exceed Human Intelligence,* New York: Penguin Books, 1999.

Rissland, Edwina, "Artificial Intelligence and Law: Stepping Stones to a Model of Legal Reasoning," *Yale Law Journal.* Vol. 99, No. 8, 1957–1981, 1990.

Susskind, Richard, *Transforming the Law: Essays on Technology, Justice and the Legal Marketplace.* New York: Oxford University Press, 2000. (See review in the appendix.)

Turtle, Howard, "Text Retrieval in the Legal World," *Artificial Intelligence and Law.* Vol. 3, No. 1–2, 5–54, 1995.

Actions

Consider attending one of the biannual conferences sponsored by the International Association for Artificial Intelligence and Law (**http://www .iaail.org**). These tend to be extremely theoretical, but practical results are often also presented, and side tutorials and workshops may be of interest. Check out a set of proceedings before making plans so you know what you're getting into. (The next chapter is a condensed version of a paper I presented at the 2005 conference in Bologna, which is among the less scientific contributions typically encountered. Feel free to skim.)

CHAPTER TWELVE

Intelligent Tools for Managing Factual Arguments

BY EXPLORING PRACTICAL QUESTIONS in the context of a supremely impractical debate, this chapter seeks to highlight the challenges and opportunities faced by those trying to promote better use of intelligent tools in the legal workplace. It lays out design features for an imagined online argument manager and describes the knowledge engineering challenges such a system presents. In addition to reviewing theoretical characteristics of factual argumentation, this chapter considers what kinds of tools are or could be available for everyday use.

Introduction

There is nothing distinctively legal about factual argumentation, but it is nonetheless critical to most legal work. Lawyers and judges constantly engage in factual analysis, even if only on a background level. Most legal matters involve some disagreement over facts.

Before we can reach conclusions on ultimate issues like responsibility and ownership, we often have to settle questions of fact. Flawless legal conclusions premised on factual errors can wreak gross miscarriages of justice. And since factual arguments can be highly persuasive even when they are fundamentally unsound, the very cause of justice requires analytical sharpness.

This chapter is based on an earlier work, Intelligent Tools for Managing Factual Arguments, in *Proceedings of the Tenth International Conference on Artificial Intelligence and Law*, Bologna, © ACM (2005) **http://doi.acm.org/10.1145/1165485.1165501**

A Case in Point: The Mysterious Mr. S.

Few writers have left behind a body of work that has engaged us as deeply as that of William Shakespeare. He is as close to a singularity as we have in world literary history.

It's odd and frustrating that we know so little about the actual person behind this name. There is a primary curiosity: Who was this person who wrote so memorably and movingly? What was he like? What did he really think? How much autobiography is encoded or reflected in the works? What learning and experiences were behind his accomplishments?

And there is a darker, secondary curiosity: Did the usual suspect in fact write the plays and poems that have come down to us as the "works of William Shakespeare"? What if it were not the man from Stratford? What if it were a *group* of people? A woman? If so, what was the rationale for pseudonymity? And how was it pulled off?

Brilliant people have bent their minds around these issues, from all sides and angles. It is a venerable debate that I find deeply fascinating. It can be maddeningly sophomoric, with much enthusiastic jumping to unwarranted conclusions and repetition of exploded fallacies. But there are also deliciously rich dimensions.

Many otherwise educated people are blissfully unaware of this controversy. Those who know of it often scoff at the idea. In some circles, simply to express openness to authorship alternatives is to declare oneself a fool or infidel.

Of course, this debate is of utterly no practical significance. Unless you believe in vindicating some uncredited writer who's looking down upon us from above. (And whoever he was, he saw fit to disguise himself pretty well, neglecting opportunities to leave behind better clues. This master of characterization and disguise deftly painted himself out of the picture.)

Nor is it of great literary or historical importance, belonging perhaps with questions like "Where was the historical Troy?" "Was Abraham Lincoln gay?" and "Who was Jack the Ripper?"

Nonetheless, it is a compelling whodunit, a wonderful detective story. It's a great example of a complex factual argument. And it's a useful foil against which to explore legal knowledge tool themes.

A Personal Journey

I've been intrigued (some might say obsessed) with the authorship question for a long time. It grows out of a lifelong love of Shakespeare. I have read many, but never all, of the plays multiple times and have seen them performed. I gave a high school course on them as a student teacher. I grab every opportunity to see films based on the plays. I plodded through tomes like Harold Bloom's *Shakespeare: The Invention of the Human*, wincing with disappointment when that arch "Bardolator" concluded that we can never hope to learn what our mutual hero really was like or thought. While attending a conference in Warwick in 2002, I made the obligatory pilgrimage to Stratford-upon-Avon, standing in the "birthplace" and believing for the moment that I was on sacred ground.

I had long been vaguely aware that the man from Stratford's authorship had been denied in favor of candidates like Francis Bacon, or even Queen Elizabeth, but I filed such theories along with those by crackpots who believe, for instance, that the U.S. moon landing was staged. Even though I knew that the Stratfordians were challenged not only by Baconians but by Marlovians and Oxfordians, I especially perked up when a distinguished academic friend casually described himself as falling into the latter camp.

Then I made the mistake of borrowing a book called *Alias Shakespeare* from my local public library.

Here was an ostensibly respectable author laying out persuasive arguments in favor of an eccentric aristocrat (Edward de Vere, the seventeenth Earl of Oxford) as the true author. He presented a plausible narrative of pseudonymity that seemed at last to deliver a satisfying story behind the miraculous works. He enlisted fellow anti-Stratfordians like Walt Whitman, Mark Twain, and Sigmund Freud, and reported on a vibrant scholarly tradition of Oxfordianism.

I read the book again. And again. It made sense. How could this be? How could this compelling explanation have eluded mainstream consciousness (or at least mine) for so long? Or had it in fact been thoroughly debunked by those who know better?

I ran the idea by various friends. Most reacted with bemused disinterest. Some turned out to be closet non-Stratfordians themselves. One responded with contempt and ridicule, as though I had hit a primal Anglo-Saxon nerve. This virulence was soon to be seen elsewhere. My new-found confidence was shaken, and I felt compelled to dig deeper, beginning with the Web.

As you might expect, the Web is crawling with material on the authorship controversy. I learned that in some online circles, it is so inflammatory that it is regarded as the "forbidden topic." I found all kinds of arguments pro and con and the various "contenders" (an inappropriate term, of course, since the dead don't contend.)

At that point I realized I had no choice but to read the entire works, trying to bear in mind the authorship question as I did so. Many happy moments in 2003 were spent working through 3,400+ pages of small print in *The Norton Shakespeare*.

Along the way, I also read several dozen books that deal implicitly or explicitly with the authorship question, from all perspectives. (Well over four thousand such books were already in print by the middle of the twentieth century.) My opinions and suspicions have fluctuated wildly. I read the collected plays of Christopher Marlowe to see if I could persuade myself that he faked his death and went on to a nominally posthumous career under a more famous pen name. (Nope.) I sampled a wide variety of surrounding Elizabethan literature, read about the production of the King James Bible, reread Homer and Ovid, and began working through the ancient Greek plays that seemed to be so influential on Shakespeare.

After finishing the collected works, I started reading a leading current dictionary of Shakespearian vocabulary word for word. (I had previously read a more specialized dictionary, Eric Partridge's *Shakespeare's Bawdy*.) Digesting an alphabetical array of Shakespeare's words, with illustrative quotes, is like going through shards of stained glass at a bombed-out cathedral and trying to reconstruct the scenes the windows depicted.

Not to hide the ball, as of this writing I don't find any of the theories entirely persuasive and have become almost as fascinated by the structure of the debate, which brings me to the present subject matter. If I were forced to make a bet, I would likely say that Oxford was indeed the primary author. Although Mr. Shakspere[1] from Stratford might well have made creative contributions to the works, while also serving as the front man, he is unlikely to have been the genius we seek.

---

[1] This was a common and phonetically accurate spelling of that man's name—the first syllable other times written "Shags," "Shacks," or "Shax."

It comes down to which authorship narrative is less *im*probable. None are without their problems. But, in my view, to dismiss the authorship *question* today borders on intellectual dishonesty.

Sample Theories

To set up the discussion below, let's review just a tiny sampling of the competing theories and proffered arguments. What person or persons actually put pen to paper in the creative efforts behind the plays and poems? Who *did* what when? Who *knew* what when? (Warning: Here and in much of what follows I am *not* purporting to be rigorous. In fact, I'm being careless. My goal is merely to give you a flavor of the argument. Complete coverage of even one strand would be utterly impossible in a short chapter.)

The Mainstream View

A first thing to recognize is that the conventional narrative is largely a construction. Yes, there unquestionably was a William Shakspere who was born (1564) and died (1616) in Stratford. We know about his parents, marriage, children, real estate purchases, lawsuits, and last testament. And yes, he was almost certainly the same man who showed up as a theatrical businessman in London by the 1590s. Prefatory material in the initial collection of plays—the First Folio published in 1623—implies that this man was the author. And the monument to him in a Stratford church pretty unambiguously takes the same position.

But—there is shockingly little other evidence supporting that conclusion, and lots of reasons to doubt it. We don't know how this man would have learned all that Shakespeare seems to have known, read all that Shakespeare clearly read, and written all that Shakespeare evidently wrote. Shakspere probably attended his local grammar school, which offered a good education in Latin, but records are lost. He did not enroll in any university and is not known to have traveled outside England. We don't know how or where he gained access to rare books, courtly and military life, aristocratic sports, legal nuances, or fine points of Italian culture.

Shakespeare the man was not paid much attention to for the century after his death, and when people began looking, the trail had gone cold. Basic demographics were soon established, but no manuscripts, books, letters, or other artistic materials could be located. Exhaustive mining of public records later yielded glimpses of commercial wheeling and dealing, but no literary life.

Despite the paucity of material, hundreds of thick biographies of the Bard have appeared, piling rumor upon conjecture and inflating the whole thing with reckless imagination. Many are quite ridiculous, some are more responsible. A recent example of the latter is Stephen Greenblatt's *Will in the World*.

In a passage typical of this genre (p. 149), Greenblatt writes, "Then sometime in the mid-1580s (the precise date is not known), he tore himself from his family, left Stratford-upon-Avon, and made his way to London." The precise date?! It would be much closer to the truth to say that *we have no idea* what Shakspere did in those years. There are some tantalizing clues and possibilities, such as the presence of a "William Shakeshaft" as a tutor in a Lancashire Catholic household and a Stratfordian's enrollment in an army in the Netherlands. But exhaustive scholarly efforts have been unable to deliver reliable evidence of *any* experiences that might account for the prodigious learning and experience so manifest in the works. Genius alone can't explain it.

That, of course, does not mean that it didn't happen.

Reasons for Doubt

More striking than the absence of confirming evidence are the many counterindications. Here are some of the leading objections to the traditional view.

They fall into two main categories: difficulties in squaring the works with the known facts of Shakspere's life and remarkable linkages to known facts in the lives of other people.

The author (whoever he or she was, or they were):

- Employs a vocabulary twice that of John Milton
- Had access to unpublished sources and made use of books not yet translated into English or Latin
- Displays lots of inside knowledge about courtly life (vocabulary, contemporary intrigues) and upper-class activities (falconry, archery, tennis, bowling)
- Shows a subtle knowledge of Italy, music, law, heraldry, horticulture, seamanship, and many esoteric subjects
- Evinces an aristocratic perspective (noble characters tend to be complex; commoners tend to be shallow, humorous, or mob-like; feudal values are emphasized over those of the emerging commercial class)

♦ Parodies powerful people, like Lord Burghley (Queen Elizabeth's right-hand man, evident model for Polonius in *Hamlet*)

♦ Comes across as an omnisexual connoisseur, well versed in all manner of encounters, paid and unpaid

As noted, William Shakspere of Stratford attended grammar school at most. His parents, wife, and children were marginally literate at best. He was married at age eighteen to a woman eight years his senior, already pregnant, and had three children. He would have been in his late twenties at the time several major poems and a dozen plays had been written. He never once spelled his name "Shake-speare," the hyphenated form often used to refer to the author. His death in 1616 went largely unnoticed. His will referenced no books, instruments, or writings.

How a struggling actor could find time, energy, and illumination to write the voluminous works in a pre-Starbucks, expensive-candles, word-processor-less world is just part of the mystery. To add some incendiary points by Charlton Ogburn (1992):

♦ There is no evidence that Shakspere ever owned a book of any kind.

♦ We know of no occasion on which a man identified as Shakespeare *the writer* was present.

♦ We know of no communication, oral or written, to such a man. No commendatory lyrics by or about him were published in his lifetime.

♦ No one in Stratford who could have known Shakspere or his descendants is ever reported to have described him as an actor *or* playwright.

♦ Every last scrap of paper that would have told us who Shakespeare actually was seems to have vanished.

A Leading Alternative Candidate

Francis Bacon was for a while the leading candidate, but some fifty others have been put forth.[2] Today, the best case seems to be made for Edward de Vere, the seventeenth Earl of Oxford (1550–1604):

♦ He came from an ancient lineage (William the Conqueror married a de Vere).

---

[2] See Mitchell (1996) for an even-handed review of the main choices.

- He received degrees from Oxford and Cambridge.
- He was a favorite of the queen (for a while).
- He was an acclaimed athlete, musician, poet, and playwright.
- He was disgraced in various ways, slummed in theaters, and owned a theatrical company.
- He stopped writing under his own name around the time (1593) the first work published under the name Shakespeare appeared (*Venus and Adonis*, referred to in its dedication as the "first heir of my invention").
- He had some thirty literary works dedicated to him.

Oxfordians make additional points:

- "Shakespeare" was referred to in the past tense several times after early 1600s.
- None of the works are conclusively dateable after 1603.
- Pen names were employed by some nobles.
- Oxford's crest had an English lion shaking a broken lance.
- A 1578 Latin dedication to Oxford used a phrase that can be translated into English as "Thy will shakes spears."
- He appears to have been nicknamed "Willie."
- After his death in 1604, King James had eight of the plays produced at court in his honor.

Biographical Echoes

Each of the camps finds plentiful echoes of the lives of their candidates in the works. For William Shakspere, it is pointed out that he had a family friend and son named Hamnet and that the plays contain references to local Warwickshire plants, customs, and leather working (his father's trade).

Greenblatt's 2004 book takes an admittedly conjectural approach to linking the probable facts of Shakspere's life to the author, emphasizing the Catholicism of family and friend recusants as the reason for keeping a low profile and, along with the deaths of father and son, as underlying a skeptical, pained attitude that resulted in the "strategic opacity" and "excision of motive" in the later plays.[3]

---

[3] *Will in the World* reads as though no one had ever raised any authorship question. But in a *Harvard* magazine (September–October 2004) article, Professor Greenblatt said that the process of writing a new Shakespeare biography "has made me respect that preposterous fantasy [alterna-

For Edward de Vere, it is noticed that he was a ward of Lord Burghley and married his daughter, that (prefiguring *Hamlet*) he was captured by pirates on the Channel, and he had a trusted cousin by the name of Horatio. In a jealous fit over imagined infidelity, he condemned his wife and refused to see her for several years. Many plots in the plays are uncannily mappable to known episodes in de Vere's life.

The sonnets, likely written at least in part to the Earl of Southampton, another ward, who Burghley sought to marry to de Vere's daughter, and dated by most to the early 1590s, describe an old man of high birth who had suffered some scandal, urging procreation upon a youth in whom he himself has a romantic interest: "When forty winters shall besiege *thy* brow" (2); "[my glass shows me] Beated and chopp'd with tann'd antiquity." (62) Consider also the autumnal flavor of the late tragedies, with meditations on extreme old age and flawed patriarchy.

In 1592, Will Shakspere was 28, de Vere 42. If traditional accounts are true, Shakspere was a rising star of the London stage. De Vere had squandered most of his inheritance, wasted his world-class education, pissed off the queen, hung out with thugs, and was accused of being a pedophile. By many accounts, he was quite a disreputable chap. Or at least a wanton voluptuary.

The sonnets also imply that their author needed to remain anonymous, but they toy with the reader:

- "My name be buried where my body is" (72)
- "<u>every</u> word doth almost tell my name" (76)

The legal and Italian dimensions are particularly interesting.

Law

No lawyer can read the works without noticing the frequent use of legal terms and concepts. They demonstrate both astonishing aptness and subtlety. Whole books have been written on their accuracy or lack thereof. My impression is that current scholarly consensus favors the former.

---

tive authorship]—if I may say so—rather more than when I began . . . because I have now taken several years of hard work and 40 years of serious academic training to grapple with the difficulty of making the connections meaningful and compelling between the life of this writer and the works that he produced." Unfortunately, in response to a letter to the editor in the next issue, Greenblatt reverted to derisive dismissiveness, asserting that Oxford could not possibly have been the author since many great plays were written after 1604—a highly debatable conclusion largely built on the self-fulfilling dating of plays based on the life of Mr. Shakspere! But now *I'm* being polemical . . .

Shakspere's father was the bailiff of Stratford at one point, and both were involved in various legal transactions and lawsuits. There is a tradition that Will might have apprenticed as a law clerk, but no documents that such a person would frequently have witnessed have ever come to light with his name on them, despite exhaustive search.

Edward de Vere was enrolled at the Inns of Court, underwent dramatic litigation over his legitimacy, and participated in many other suits and transactions.

Italy

Italian venues and themes likewise flood the works. Scholars point to remarkable topographical exactitude, deep borrowings from the *commedia dell arte*, and seeming awareness of people and practices in contemporary Italy not known to have been available in publications.

Shakspere is not believed ever to have traveled outside England or known Italian. But he may have been friends with linguist John Florio.

Edward de Vere traveled extensively in Italy, where he was a guest at aristocratic households. He spoke and read Italian.

Why and How (Theory of the Case)

Supreme Court Justice John Paul Stevens, a declared Oxfordian, complained that advocates of that position lack "a single, coherent theory of the case." Such a theory needs to answer why and how, among other things.

Why would de Vere disguise himself?

- Conduct unbecoming to a noble?
- Cover for controversy?
- Orders from the queen? As paid Tudor propagandist? ("art made tongue-tied by authority")
- Protect Southampton?
- Literary delight?

How could he have gotten away with it?

- Obscurity?
- Patronage?

♦ Bribery?

♦ The fog of time?

Debates like this go on forever because they can't be definitively settled, and no one has the power or resources to bring them to a binding conclusion, unlike some legal disputes. It is possible but unlikely that significant new evidence will arise in the authorship debate. Until then, it is predominantly a matter of sorting through and interpreting existing material.

How Technology Could Help

In the course of the above explorations, I found myself yearning for an organized, comprehensive summary of the facts and theories. Surely *someone* must have made it their business to marshal the better points on all sides into an objective framework.

So far I haven't found such a thing. Some books and Web sites do better than others in dispassionately covering the theories, but none approach what seems possible with contemporary technology. The authorship-debate community appears to be just as barren of intelligent argument-management tools as the legal profession.

Suppose one wanted to construct an ideal environment for organizing the authorship claims. What might such a thing look like? It would probably be a shared resource accessible over the Internet. It would be a complete and easily navigable argument space—one that is also personalizable and annotatable. It would be easy to use and support a range of alternative viewpoints. Let's dub it a Simple Holistic Argument Kiosk, or SHAK.

What might such a kiosk do?

Keeping Track

At the most basic, we would like conventional database functionality. Just keeping track—or keeping score—is helpful. Having places to put questions and open issues keeps them in front of us. We'd like to have an easily searchable compilation of the following:

♦ What factual theories have been put forth

♦ What arguments have been made

♦ What points are established and disputed

♦ Who asserted/rejected/refuted what when

The structured recording of such information would allow us to see quickly whether anyone seriously contests a given point and efficiently be informed or reminded about established errors.

While the argument collection for our topic is being constructed, it would be handy to record questions, such as, "Are there known examples of Elizabethan staged deaths, like that which some suppose happened in Marlowe's case?"

We'd clearly want to be able to lodge *un*knowns in the argument structure—things for which there is not yet evidence or plausible argument one way or the other. Just the fact that something *is* unknown is often important knowledge.

For any statement, we typically have a theory of what the utterer knew and intended. When William Basse wrote, "He dyed in April 1616" regarding his poem about Spencer, Chaucer, and Beaumont making room in their tomb for Shakespeare, was he misled, deliberately contributing to a cover-up, or properly informed?

One would want the ability to lodge suggestions, observations, considerations, and other kinds of annotations anywhere anytime. And in a multiuser context, such annotations ought to be private or public at the option of the user.

A SHAK would need to store probabilities—how likely X is in Y's opinion—and support different perspectives. The ability to represent multiple inconsistent views simultaneously is critical.

Prompting Us

Putting aside some intelligent moves discussed later, conventional software can certainly be useful in *eliciting* things from people and organizing them into useful frameworks.

For instance, a system could guide us to do things like these:

- ♦ Tease out implicit assumptions, sub-assumptions, and open issues
- ♦ Break down compound assertions
- ♦ Identify known exceptions and undermining points
- ♦ Imagine plausible circumstances that *might* undermine a given proposition (from the infinity of potential negative assumptions that could theoretically undermine any positive statement)
- ♦ Consider what kind of evidence would make a point stronger or weaker if it were found

Showing Us

Spatial metaphors are rampant in our argumentative thinking and talking. Graphical depiction of argument structures is one effective way of seeing wholes (and seeing holes). Chains of inferences can be presented in which established and contested points are differentiated by color.

The complex attack-and-support relations among points and positions present in any nontrivial argument cannot easily be expressed in a reasonably sized two-dimensional rendering, but subsets and subregions often can be.

It would be useful to be able to see the implications of accepting or rejecting a point by having that decision ripple up a line of reasoning—and to be able to apply filters that show and hide material in the SHAK based on who contributed them, whose point of view they represent, and what topics they deal with.

Thinking for Us

To count as an "intelligent tool," SHAK would need to do more than gather, store, and display information. It would preprocess and parse content in connection with its elicitation of human input and *suggest* gaps, conflicts, and ambiguities in an accruing argument repository. An intelligent argument manager would notice patterns, generate alternative narrative scenarios, and guide us through processes of thoughtful assessment.

Broader Uses

The uses of systematic argument-landscape mapping are many. Once a comprehensive and well-structured argument framework was in place for a rich debate like the authorship controversy, all desired points could be assigned unique identifiers, and people could then tag external texts by the arguments explicitly or implicitly put forth in particular passages. You can imagine this being useful in a semantic web of Shakespeariana.

Legal Applicability

One may reasonably ask how typical an argument the Shakespeare authorship debate is. Does it illustrate issues and features generally relevant to law? Is it representative of factual controversies in the legal domain?

I think so.

Some peculiarities of the authorship debate, such as literary stylometrics and what to make of double entendres, are not often encountered in other situations. But questions of identity, knowledge, and motive are standard fare in legal disputes. What did tobacco or pharmaceutical company executives know about their products? When? Who authored an incriminating e-mail sent under a forged header? Which defendant wrote the ransom note?

Authorship, after all, is a kind of responsibility. Deciding who deserves "credit" for literary works is analytically similar to deciding who deserves blame for some civil wrong or guilt for a criminal act.

And factual arguments in legal contexts often *are* as polemical, complicated, and maddening as those in the authorship debate.

So it's fair to assume that an argument system built for contexts like the above would be straightforwardly useful for legal purposes. An online argument framework system like SHAK would, for example, find ready use by both parties and judges in actual litigation. Simply eliciting and organizing all claims, assertions, denials, and admissions in a common data structure permits rapid high-level overviews of the points in controversy. Case teams in law firms, law departments, and government agencies would find such a system immensely useful for evaluating cases and planning litigation strategy.

Design Considerations

Those who would build effective tools in this field quickly encounter challenges. Factual arguments present many interesting complexities.

There are both ontological and knowledge-engineering challenges. How do we achieve expressive coherence in a shared argument space? What kinds of representations and reasoning are needed to intelligently suggest questions or notice patterns? Can we realistically express important arguments in a canonical form, to disambiguate, ease search, and enable automated reasoning?

Data Complexity

Simple relational databases don't work well for capturing argument frameworks because many of their most important features are not effectively expressed in table structures. While balancing tests based on weighted multifactor analysis may be appropriate for local contexts, the overall posture of an argument involves more complex configurations of elements. Single points, for instance, can cut different ways in different contexts or in the hands of different arguers.

Complexity also arises from quantity. My guess is that there are on the order of ten thousand discrete factual points at play in the authorship debate.

Competing Agendas

Arguments can serve two broad but competing goals: reaching knowledge and achieving persuasion. Truth seeking and opinion shaping are not typically both pursued at the same time. They involve different motives and vocabularies.

Often people honestly argue to know what the best position is. They want to accumulate points and considerations so that there can be progress, not repetition. Quarantining fallacious arguments can defang them and counter demagoguery. Debate can clarify differences, suggest places to *look* for evidence.

From the truth-seeking, investigatory perspective, it's helpful to have sound argumentative bookkeeping. Tools can help us deal with the fact that even when good faith is present all around, and even when people agree on the power of specific points and the soundness of local arguments, they may disagree about larger structures, combinations, and conclusions.

Achieving persuasion or rhetorical advantage involves different motives. As debaters, we'd like to know "what points we should be prepared to parry." A SHAK would be useful for defensive argument management by helping us not make claims that can easily be rebutted. From an offensive posture, we'd like to engage in intelligent discovery of potential counterarguments and weak points. No one likes being blindsided or made a fool of.

Both kinds of argumentation deal with many of the same challenges and can be served by similar tools. In both contexts it is useful to bound the arena of debate and clear out argumentative underbrush when sub-branches can be pruned because higher level undercuts have been accepted.

Tools designed for rhetorical advantage may involve some features not needed for investigatory purposes—for example, guidance on what kinds and sequences of arguments are empirically most likely to be persuasive. But even when you are managing arguments for the sake of advocacy, when you are scoring debaters' points rather than seeking truth, you are well advised to figure out what actually happened, or at least what one would be most justified in believing happened.

Facts vs. Values vs. Norms and Time

Arguments about facts are usually distinguished from those about rules, norms, and values. They deal with matters of what is (or was), with ontology, rather than aesthetics, politics, or ethics. They don't involve the deontic modalities of obligation, prohibition, and permission. Personal preferences and aversions don't—or at least shouldn't—enter into the conversation.

From a point-counterpoint modeling perspective, though, fact arguments are not that different from other kinds. There are almost always factual dimensions to policy and ethical arguments. And there are normative aspects *within* factual arguments, such as standards of proof and conventions of taking turns.

Within the world of facts, the time dimension turns out to make little difference. There are structural similarities in discussing what *has* happened, what *is* happening, and what *will* likely happen if X is done. Predictive arguments, in other words, are not that different from historical ones— what is likely *to* happen involves similar inferences to what is likely to *have happened*. Questions of tactics, strategy, and effectiveness (what works), of what "should" be done as a matter of practical efficacy, also belong in the factual camp, because ultimately they have to do with how the world works.

Messiness

Most factual argumentation is rather messy. That is, it is not straightforwardly reportable as the simple exchange of well-structured propositions and logical claims.

There is much performative, communicative activity going on when people argue, whether ostensibly for pure truth-seeking purposes or for opinion shaping. There is the Schadenfreude of seeing an opponent's argument implode. The use of various kinds of debate tricks. The politics of characterization, such as guilt by association and ad hominem attacks.

Most real-world arguments exhibit partisan tendencies to exaggerate, disregard nuance, and rely on shoddy intelligence. The Shakespeare authorship controversy, for instance, often displays an appallingly low quality of debate.

Arguments that something should be accepted because of who asserted it, or that something should be rejected because of the invalidity of something else said by its assertor (arguments from *lack* of authority?), deserve to be ferreted out and labeled as such. One way is to make their dubious premises explicit.

The allegedly improper motivations of someone offering an interpretative or analytical position are usually quite irrelevant. A common move by Stratfordians has been to assert that claims of aristocratic authorship are motivated by the snobbish view that only an upper-class person *could* have had the talent to be Shakespeare and that to question the plausibility of someone from the gentry writing his works is to display class arrogance. On the other hand, a common move by anti-Stratfordians is to accuse academic defenders of snobbishly rejecting alternative viewpoints because "amateurs" can't perform sound scholarship.

In complex arguments, even a single person's belief system often includes two alternative (and possibly incompatible) propositions supporting some other propositions, or just some open questions. What emerges are several internally consistent scenarios or theories, and one is left having to judge their respective plausibility. Often this takes the form of dueling generalizations.

Process and State

One challenge-*reducing* aspect of a project like SHAK is that it need not deal with the *procedural* aspects of argumentation. The focus is on the argument's declarative aspects, its synchronic rather than its diachronic dimensions. We need not model the history of the "game" or the rules by which it is played to have a useful account of its current state. From a practical point of view, even if multiple parties are permitted to add and edit content, an appointed Keeper of the Frame or SHAK Master can resolve discrepancies about what is allowed to go where.

Pointillism

One minimal feature of any SHAK would be a clear representation of points and their relations. We expect a lucid depiction of "point space."

Varieties and Properties of Points

For maximal expressive power, it would seem that a SHAK would encourage and support high specificity and granularity in the points expressed.

Perfect atomicity may not be achievable, but there should be means to distinguish *simple* from *compound*.

The likelihood of a statement being true, or the degree of confidence we should have in it, can depend on the specificity of a point. We can assert propositions about properties of the author that stop short of his identity, such as "The author was a native-born Englishman."

There are freestanding points as well as those that consist in supporting or pointing out some defect in another point. Explanations are one kind of supporting argument ("X did Y because a and b . . .").

Whether a point is controverted or accepted should be separately recordable for each person or perspective whose views are represented in the system.

Aboutness

An effective point-management system needs to be particularly good at modeling *aboutness*—what an argument is about, what a particular point is about. The date or period referred to, and the people or objects involved, are elementary subjects naturally tracked. But often the subject of a point can and should be specified at a much more subtle level.

Some points have as their referents postulated circumstances in a real world, while others are about other points. Some make statements about an object world and some about the point world.

And when a point is contested, it's important to be precise as to what *about* that point is contested. The very subject tags (who, when) can be in contention.

The subjects of discourse in factual argumentation include states and events of the physical world, but more often human actions, especially speech acts. They include epistemological states such as knowledge and intent.

Interpoint Logic

Mapping the support-and-attack relationships among argument points involves a different level or layer of representation.

A single given fact can be used both to support and undermine a proposition, typically through intermediate assertions. Likewise, different combinations of accepted points can be claimed to justify the same given conclusion.

Given a collection of points, and specified reasoning techniques, it should be possible to automate cascades of inferences. Some of those techniques will involve stock arguments, or argument patterns, such as that certain kinds of conclusions can be drawn from the absence of evidence or from someone's failure to act (like no one going after the many pirated works and misattributions in Shakespeare's case).

As a manager or user of an online argument facility, one will be called upon not only to take a position on specific points but on general principles of reasoning, such as how much weight to accord a particular kind of factor.

Tools in Use or On the Way

Contemporary Legal Practice

My informal impression, based on years of observing practitioners and keeping up with the legal tech trade literature, is that very few lawyers use *any* significant technology to help them organize arguments. The most common tools remain yellow pads and word processors.

Some litigators use specialized outliners like GrandView, Ecco, and NoteMap to organize their trial planning. And some take advantage of evidence-organizing features in litigation-support products, like Summation (**http://www.summation.com**). Summation's Case Organizer gives you the ability to place case data (transcribed testimony, document records, images, etc.) and your own comments into an outline-style staging area. Similar features can be found in case-management products like Time Matters, recently acquired by LexisNexis.

Custom Applications

I've set forth several times to build element/evidence/argument analyzers, which long ago struck me as obvious tools that lawyers should find handy. The idea of using software to elicit the claims and counterclaims involved in a dispute, specify their logical elements, and link those elements to actual and potential evidence pro and con is an old one.

One law firm engaged my company to build a custom trial planner application using CAPS. They wanted a shared repository of analysis, issues, evidence, and notes for teams of lawyers and paralegals involved in complex litigation. Rather than passing around versions of a Word document only one person could edit at a time, they requested an easily navigable, multiuser framework. Such an application was successfully deployed. But I was astonished there hadn't been a readily handy commercial alternative. Some colleagues and I invested a great deal of time in the mid-1990s plotting (but not pursuing) a robust generic application along these lines.

CaseMap

The best example of successful software offering some of the features we seek is CaseMap, from CaseSoft (later acquired by LexisNexis). CaseMap is now the leading commercial software package for case analysis and litigation strategy. It greatly eases the job of recording and manipulating the facts, entities, and issues involved in a case. Tens of thousands of law offices and government agencies—from solo practitioners to the ninety-plus United States Attorneys' Offices—have been licensed.

You can think of CaseMap as a special-purpose spreadsheet or database, with preconfigured structures for entities, relationships, and operations commonly encountered in the litigation context. It makes it easy to compile witness lists and chronologies and to cross-correlate pieces of evidence with issues. It anticipates and solves many practical issues encountered in computer-aided case analysis, such as handling inexact dates and date ranges and producing nicely formatted summaries of issues, players, and facts for clients to review.

CaseSoft has made an admirable contribution not just in the form of tools but in the form of methods and education. It regularly publishes useful articles on case analysis and brainstorming. Its installed base of enthusiastic users ensures that the product and associated methods continue to evolve.

I used CaseMap early on to help me understand the authorship issue, using it to manage a list of "objects" (people, places, things) and to display an annotated timeline of key events, using the companion TimeMap software.

As useful as CaseMap is, it lacks some key features I would see as necessary in SHAK. CaseMap has few tools for mapping complex relationships among arguments, does not run on the Web, performs no logical calculations, and includes no reports to show chains of reasoning, let alone graphical displays of claim networks.

Knowledge Mappers

At least two striking products venture into areas largely untouched by previous commercial legal technologies. They both offer promising applicability to factual-argument management.

Attenex Patterns

Attenex Corporation (**www.attenex.com**, pronounced ah-TEN-ex) focuses on achieving a tenfold increase in productivity in document-intensive processes in the legal profession. Its Patterns product uses natural language processing, computational linguistics, latent semantic analysis, and information visualization techniques to enable such productivity. Chief technology officer Skip Walter talks of "documents that describe themselves and find their friends." Patterns has largely been applied in the burgeoning e-discovery world but has remarkable promise for automated pattern recognition and rich visualization in other contexts, like fraud detection in financial transactions and social network mapping based on e-mail repositories.

I suspect that Patterns might yield interesting results if its text-analysis utilities were applied against Shakespeare's works and extant writings by the various proposed authors—one could compare the resulting conceptual fingerprints. But it also could be a handy tool for mapping and navigating through the voluminous materials and arguments *about* authorship. Just as litigation paralegals can use it to quickly mark documents as relevant/irrelevant or privileged work product, amateur (and professional) literary historians might use Patterns to sort through and characterize points favoring different authorship theories. Then when one wanted to see, for example, all of the best points in favor of, say, Sir Walter Raleigh, those could instantly be highlighted in color while still displayed in their natural conceptual contexts.

LawSaurus

Minnesota-based Pritchard Law Webs is developing an innovative product called LawSaurus, described as "a thesaurus-based authoring, editing, and publishing environment for polyhierarchically organized networks of related information." Its initial application context is a legal information portal (**www.lawmoose.com**), where online resources about law and lawyers can be linked to terms in a rich taxonomy, but it offers a stunningly generic architecture for any information-management problem that can be expressed relationally.

A SHAK-like environment using LawSaurus could exploit its ability to build freeform networks of nodes and links. By defining relations both generic to argumentation (this point is supported/undermined by that point, accepted/rejected by that person) and specific to the authorship controversies (this person knew that person, this work seems to have used that work as source), one could code a rich array of information to associatively browse and annotate.

So far as I know, Pritchard does not intend to implement automated analysis of LawSaurus networks, but they would seem straightforwardly processable into data structures that *could* be mined for telltale patterns and used as fodder for reasoning.

SHAKy Conclusions

Is the idea of a fair and open argument space a rationalist illusion? For most important questions, aren't there just too many rhetorical and analytical twists to contain? Can IT and AI really help us better manage that complexity? I'm convinced they can.

We survived an election in the United States where an administration was reelected in part by exploiting the right-wing pseudopopulism that was on the rise. That movement ironically mirrored aspects of the Islamic extremism it condemned. The arguments behind these world-threatening ideologies, of course, have not been primarily factual ones. But there and elsewhere the paucity of tools shapes the landscape of behavior. The lack of good argument-management technology advantages those who are more rhetorically adept (or unprincipled, ruthless, Machiavellian).

Most legal (and literary-historical) controversies aren't quite so apocalyptic. And let's face it, if arguments were totally fair, they wouldn't be nearly as much fun. But we can also have fun while fairly discussing serious issues.

Who wrote Shakespeare? I still don't know. I'd feel more comfortable in my ignorance if I could reliably access the best thinking on all facets of that controversy in a comprehensive framework. But what I'd *really* like is to see tools of that sort used regularly for law's purposes on today's world stage.

Epilogue

While the original version of this chapter was undergoing last revisions, I finally read Alan Nelson's recent biography of de Vere. This sober tour through the documentary evidence and surrounding events doesn't help Oxfordians. The seventeenth earl's many surviving letters and reports by contemporaries depict a self-obsessed, venal hooligan. His attributed poems are mediocre, his degrees apparently titular. Once in a great while there is a vaguely Shakespearian cadence in his correspondence, and there remain many eerie biographical resonances with Shakespeare's works. I can accept that great artists can be awful people and that transcendent artistry can coexist with buffoonery and banality (consider Mozart or Sinatra). But de Vere's authorship now strained my credulity as much as Mr. Shakspere's. At least until I read John Anderson's *Shakespeare by Another Name*, which makes a good case for Oxford . . .

Going Deeper

Anderson, Mark, *Shakespeare by Another Name,* New York: Gotham Books, 2006.

Bloom, Harold, *Shakespeare: The Invention of the Human*, New York: Riverhead Books, 1998.

Frank, Thomas, *What's the Matter with Kansas? How Conservatives Won the Heart of America*, New York: Metropolitan Books, 2004.

Greenblatt, Stephen, *Will in the World*, New York: W.W. Norton, 2004.

Greenblatt, S., W. Cohen, J. Howard, and K. Maus, K, *The Norton Shakespeare*, New York: W.W. Norton, 1997.

Greenspun, P., and M. Lauritsen, Making Way for Intelligence in Case Space, In *Proceedings of the Fifth International Conference on Artificial Intelligence and Law*, College Park, MD, June 1995.

Mitchell, John, *Who Wrote Shakespeare?* London: Thames and Hudson, 1996.

Nelson, Alan, *Monstrous Adversary. The Life of Edward de Vere, 17th Earl of Oxford*, Liverpool: Liverpool University Press, 2003.

Ogburn, Charlton, *The Mysterious William Shakespeare. The Myth and the Reality*. McLean, VA: EPM, 1992.

Partridge, Eric, *Shakespeare's Bawdy*, 3rd ed., London: Routledge Classics, 1968.

Sobran, Joseph, *Alias Shakespeare*, New York: Free Press, 1997.

CHAPTER THIRTEEN

The Web as Knowledge Tool

eLawyering

The term *eLawyering* refers to lawyers doing their work using the Web and associated electronic networking technologies. This includes new ways to communicate and collaborate with clients, prospective clients, and other lawyers (both within and beyond an office), assemble documents, settle disputes, and manage legal knowledge. Think of a lawyering "verb," and there are corresponding electronic-network tools and techniques.

Some of these correspondences are summarized in the following table:

Lawyer Actions	eLawyering Analogs
Interview	Online questionnaires
Investigate	Online factual research
Research	Online legal research
Analyze	Online expert systems
Draft	Web-based document assembly
Counsel	Online advice systems
Negotiate	Online dispute resolution
Collaborate	Web conferencing Virtual deal rooms and "war rooms"
Manage	Case-management extranets Web-based document management
Market	Websites
Learn/teach	E-learning

Merely using online resources for factual and legal research is hardly new. Forms of that go back over twenty years. But the richness and scope of available resources on the modern Web are substantially different. And even though marketing Web sites, e-learning, and online dispute resolution have also been with us for a while, they, too, are evolving fast. Finally, phenomena like online advice systems, Web-based document preparation, and virtual court proceedings are only now beginning to be seen in earnest.

While they constitute just a subset of the vast legal technology world, eLawyering and its lawyer-less analogs present fundamental challenges for our profession. There are dangers, but also great opportunities. For instance, in five years, small law firms might well lose most of the routine legal services market to legal information companies, retaining a foothold only in litigation and certain lines of customized advice. By then, alternative providers, with more sophisticated technology, may also be serving corporate counsel with interactive solutions that are more cost effective than traditional lawyering.

eLawyering in Connection with the Courts

Many forms of eLawyering, of course, do not involve any interaction with the judicial system or court-like entities. Lawyers in transactional practices can engage in many forms of Web-enabled services without touching any court. Even litigators can pursue many eLawyering activities independently of the judiciary, such as online client interactions and e-discovery exchanges and operations. They can (and largely still do) also interact with the courts in non-electronic modes.

But there are many *intersections* of e-lawyering with e-courts. The now commonly recognized categories, associated with their pre-Web analogs, are as follows:

Lawyer Action	eLawyering Analog
File documents	E-filing
Serve documents	E-service
Access docket information and case records	Online docket and file access
Appear in court (courtroom or chambers)	Virtual hearings

What about the Lawyer-less E-litigants?

One of the great challenges of the contemporary court system is that of self-represented litigants. And one of the most interesting dimensions of e-lawyering is the opportunity it presents to serve people—not necessarily traditional "clients"—in new ways.

Commercial entities—both associated and unassociated with law firms—have emerged to serve the huge latent market for reasonably priced, good-quality legal information and software. Why bother with a traditional firm if you can get divorce papers, wills, or other consumer legal services over the Internet? Or telephonic help at a low fixed fee? Non-lawyer legal information Web sites have now processed tens of thousands of transactions.

In most jurisdictions, lawyers themselves can ethically offer "unbundled" legal services, where they provide less than the full bundle of traditional representation. Ghostwriting and coaching are two examples. Web-based techniques like online interviews and automated document drafting can make unbundled services radically more cost effective. Here the litigant chooses to go with "less lawyer" rather than "no lawyer."

Nonprofit legal services organizations across the country have mounted statewide Web sites laden with legal information, and many now offer free interactive forms. These are available for traditional advocates, limited representation cases, and self help.

Legal Cybernautics

Besides its implications for the future of equal justice—and lawyers' paychecks—elawyering unites strands of cutting-edge research, development, and business innovation that stretch back decades. The rising generation of lawyers will be beneficiaries—or victims—of long-simmering work in ultrahigh-speed electronic communications, ubiquitous connectivity, advanced user interfaces, and artificial intelligence. That generation will seize—or give way to—dramatic new business models for delivering professional services, championed by aggressive entrepreneurs.

So a central question is how lawyers can best navigate and prosper in this new space of technical and business opportunities. How can we be effective "cybernauts"? What skills do we need to learn, and unlearn? How can and should the role of the law school change? Where will law firms, legal departments, and courts find the seeds of their own transformations?

This all goes beyond "legal tech" and aging prognosticators, beyond geeks and geezers. Now is a time for all lawyers to pay attention. This is a matter of redesigning our practices for a digital age. Of being energized, not enervated, by the winds of change. Not all of us care to master the technical details, fascinating as they can be, or ride the bucking bronco of cyber-legal entrepreneurism. But none of us can responsibly ignore the new world that is not so quietly dawning.

Digital networks have the striking property of being simultaneously subjects, tools, and locations of legal practice. Lawyers will practice *about*, *with*, and *within* such networks. No prior technology has been as radically and ubiquitously relevant to a profession. What excuse could we lawyers have for not utilizing this technology to the fullest benefit of our clients, societies, and selves?

Going Deeper

Information about the eLawyering Task Force of the Law Practice Management Section of the ABA can be found at **www.elawyering.org**.

CHAPTER FOURTEEN

Choosing Smarter

To PARAPHRASE FORREST GUMP, life is a box of choice-lets. We deal
with choices all the time, although few of us are very good at it. Psy-
chologists have identified dozens of decisional fallacies that beguile us.
And as much as we like *having* choices, we don't typically like *making*
choices.

Lawyers face choices throughout their personal and business lives. Some
choices are nearly invisible and instantaneous; others involve extended
deliberation. Some choices are made by one person alone; many involve
consultation with others.

Most choices relate to things people wish to get or do. Some involve alternative conclusions to treat as a basis for action, such as competing legal
analyses or business strategies. We often need to decide what to think,
how best to explain something, or which argument to emphasize.

Lawyer choices may relate to the substance of their work—such as
whether to file a case in state or federal court, which expert witness to put
on the stand, or whether a client's worker should be treated as an
employee or a contractor. They may also relate to the business of law practice—such as where to open a second office, who to hire, or which software package to purchase.

I've long been fascinated with choice making as a phenomenon and have
devoted a lot of time to considering how technology can help us do it better. This chapter is a summary of those ideas.

Chapter 14 is copyrighted by and included with permission from All About Choice, Inc.

Anatomy of a Choice

A decision is a special kind of problem, one that involves a reasonably defined set of issues and circumstances (and thus is different from a "mess," where the problems themselves have yet to be clearly discerned). A decision usually requires coming to a particular conclusion. It can involve figuring out what to do, how much, when, where, etc. It can encompass a number of interacting probabilities, perhaps arranged in a "decision tree." Because of their variability, there's no universal method that serves well to approach all decisions, let alone all problems.

A choice, in turn, is a special kind of decision, where you need to select from a group of discrete options. To deliberate (from the Latin *libra*, a scale or balance) is to balance alternatives. While choices come in many shapes and sizes, and can present endlessly different kinds of things among which to select, it turns out that there *are* generic methods that work well to support the distinctive forms of deliberation involved in all of them. I've come to the conclusion that a "universal grammar" underlies choice making and that understanding it can both enhance the quality of our choices and drive the design of knowledge tools to support them.

Choices have a characteristic geometry that lends itself to a three-dimensional box metaphor. One dimension is that of *options*—the things among which one is choosing. A second dimension is that of *factors*—the qualities that distinguish options from one another. A third dimension is that of *perspectives*—the different evaluative takes that one or more people can have of how the options fare on the various factors. Each option can be rated on each factor from each perspective. Imagine something like this:

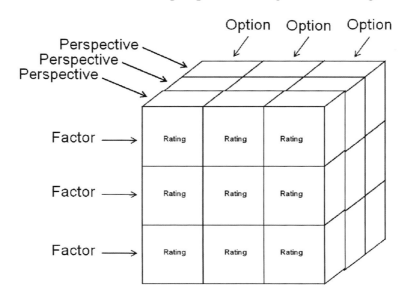

While there are many different terms for these key dimensions (for instance, *alternatives, considerations*, and *viewpoints*), all choices lend themselves quite well to being characterized in such a framework. This is hardly a surprise to anyone who has drawn a matrix of job candidates and hiring criteria on a whiteboard or organized the pros and cons of alternative legal strategies on a yellow pad. What's interesting is the rich edifice of insights and tools one can build on this geometric foundation. I will describe one such tool here to make it easier to explore the architecture of choice.

Multi-criteria Decision Making

Weighted factor analysis and related techniques for assessing options on criteria with differing degrees of relative importance have been around for a long time, and I've been working on a variation that seems to provide a substantially more powerful and easy way to deliberate about choices. By iteratively refining each of the dimensions mentioned earlier, "choice-boxing" helps deal with choice overload.

Here are some of the key concepts. (Most are simple and familiar. This abbreviated account doesn't get into all the interesting possibilities.)

Choices and Options

Choice making involves selecting from groups of alternatives. Each possible selection is an option. ("What are my options?") I use *choice* to refer to the overall decision or one of the particular selections ultimately made and *options* for the things among which one chooses.

Related terms for individual options include *candidates* and *alternatives*.

Some choices involve picking a single best option from a group; others involve picking several, or even ordering an entire set from most preferred to least.

Categories

A given choice generally involves options that share certain kinds of characteristics, making it possible to compare them in terms of common factors. Those characteristics define one or more categories of things within which one is choosing. For example, the category might be "digital camcorders," "possible birthday presents for Jane," or "rental apartments in downtown Chicago."

While every set of options can be seen as belonging to a large set of increasingly specific categories (electronic devices | video recorders | camcorders | digital camcorders), there is generally one category that best describes the set being considered.

By categorizing their choice in a standardized way, people can more easily access options, factors, and other information identified by others as worth considering in such a choice.

Factors

While a wide variety of techniques and approaches are used to make choices, they usually involve the consideration of multiple factors in terms of which the candidates differ. Factors are *kinds* of qualities or characteristics in terms of which options may be described and compared. They are answers to questions like "What makes a good ___?" and "What makes a bad ___?"

Related terms include *consideration, criterion, objective, goal, differentiator, care,* and *concern.*

Factors often have differential weights in a particular choice—the relative degree of importance or significance attached to each by each perspective being considered in a decision.

Weighted factor analysis is one common method for systematically comparing options in a choice situation. Each option is rated with respect to each factor, each rating is turned into a normalized score, and the weighted total of scores across all factors is used to reflect its relative "goodness."

Ratings

A rating is the information entered with respect to a given factor for a given option.

This term is most apt for factors that can be evaluated in quantitative terms and that involve some judgment or opinion, but you can think of it more generally as "what there is to say about this option in terms of this factor."

Related terms include *assessment, attribute, feature,* and *property.*

Scores

To fairly compare and combine ratings across different factors, and across different perspectives—in other words, for them to be commensurable—they should be normalized to a common scale. For example, the price of items may range from $300 to $3,000, and their ease of use may be judged on a scale of 1 to 5. For the respective contribution of ratings on these factors to contribute to total scores only as much as those factors are explicitly weighted—and not be affected by the units in which they may happen to be measured—they both should be converted to a common scale, such as dollars, percentage of optimality, or units of goodness. I use the word *score* to refer to the normalized value of a rating.

Perspectives

There can be more than one perspective at play in a given choice context. A sole decision maker may have more than one way of looking at the options and factors, and each member of a deciding group will typically have at least one of his or her own. Helpers may have perspectives that vary in at least some respects from the decision maker(s). There can also be perspectives of candidates, suppliers, or other "choosees."

Perspectives are distinct informational or evaluative takes on a choice. They capture different voices and viewpoints—for instance, from different people or time frames.

Each perspective can have its own view about the relative importance of the various factors and its own weight(s) relative to other perspectives (potentially differing by factor.) In other words, each *factor* has a weight *in* each perspective, and each *perspective* has a weight *for* each factor. The latter ability (to weight a perspective differently by factor) can be used, for example, to reflect someone's expertise in a certain aspect of a decision or a given user's entitlement to disproportionate impact on one or more aspects. (The managing partner might be given double weight in a hiring decision about an executive director.)

Kinds of Factors

Factors can be organized into four basic kinds based on the following:

- ◆ Whether they are objective or subjective (are ratings a matter of fact or opinion?)
- ◆ Whether their ratings can be scored, or are merely informational

Here are examples of each:

	Scored	**Informational**
Objective	price most "features" number of pixels installed base years in business	supplier name supplier Web site links to reviews
Subjective	likeability competence quality of experience ease of use	notes observations

Choiceboxes

A choicebox involves mapping one or more options, one or more factors, and one or more perspectives to imagined *x, y,* and *z* axes, respectively. The choice can be envisioned as a three-dimensional box. There is a column for each option, a row for each factor, and a layer for each perspective. (It's possible, of course, to map these dimensions differently or let users swap axes so that, for example, options are rows and factors columns.) Each cell at the intersection of such a column, row, and layer represents the characterization of some option in terms of some factor according to some perspective. There are also columns for factor and perspective weights.

Each perspective layer can have a total score row showing the weighted average of scores for all options on the factors present. When there are multiple perspectives present in a box, a summary layer is available to show weighted averages of weights, ratings/scores, and totals from across the perspectives.

For example, imagine that Jane and John are partners in a law firm that is deciding which case-management system to buy. They've narrowed it down to three products: Ace, Acme, and Apex. After lots of discussion, the choice seems to hinge on three factors: completeness of features, quality of interface, and ease of learning.

The following figure depicts how this matrix of options, factors, and perspectives might be represented in a choicebox. We're seeing Jane's perspective up front. The factors are matters of opinion, so her ratings and those of John may well differ. (In a real-world case, of course, other factors would be present, including some "objective" ones like price.) Weights and scores are omitted in these figures.

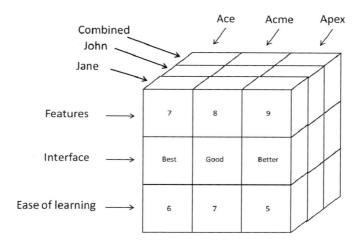

The next figure makes the separate perspective layers clearer. Now we can see some of John's different ratings and average ratings on the combined layer.

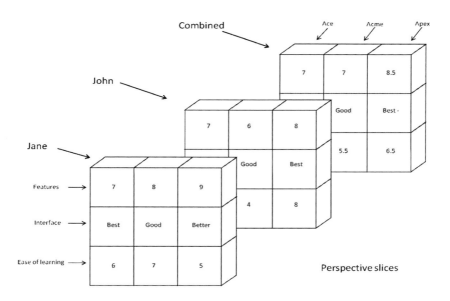

Note that the box can be "sliced" in other ways. For instance, you might want to see how a single option is rated across the several perspectives:

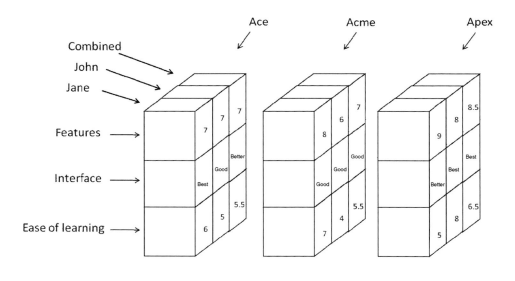

Option slices

Or you might want to see how all the options are rated on all the perspectives on a single factor:

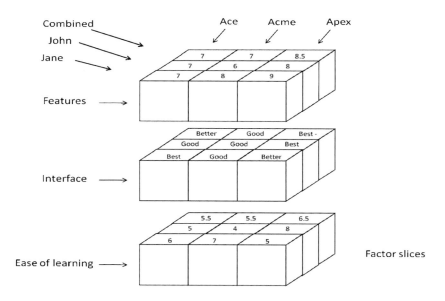

Factor slices

You can get a sense of how the options rank on each of the factors from the ratings on the various layers. Some rank first on some factors from Jane's perspective; some rank first from John's perspective. But how do they rank overall?

To complete the picture, you need to add scores and weights.

A common scoring strategy is to use percentages. Since two of the factors are expressed in a simple 0–10 scale, with 10 being best, you can just multiply the rating by 10 to get an appropriate percentage. For the interface factor, expressed in this case by words like *good* and *better*, you might associate scores with possible ratings as follows:

Best	100
Better	80
Good	70
OK	50
Bad	30
Worse	20
Worst	0

Given this setup, and adding factor weights, you can compute scores for each perspective and for the overall box like this:

	Jane	**Ace**		**Acme**		**Apex**	
weight		*rating*	*score*	*rating*	*score*	*rating*	*score*
5	**Features**	7	70	8	80	9	90
8	**Interface**	best	100	good	70	better	80
10	**Ease of learning**	6	60	7	70	5	50
	Total score for Jane		76.09		72.17		69.13

	John	**Ace**		**Acme**		**Apex**	
weight		*rating*	*score*	*rating*	*score*	*rating*	*score*
10	**Features**	7	70	6	60	8	80
5	**Interface**	good	70	good	70	best	100
2	**Ease of learning**	5	50	4	40	8	80
	Total score for John		67.65		60.59		85.88

	Combined	**Ace**		**Acme**		**Apex**	
weight		*rating*	*score*	*rating*	*score*	*rating*	*score*
7.5	**Features**	7	70	7	70	8.5	85
6.5	**Interface**	better	85	good	70	best minus	90
6	**Ease of learning**	5.5	55	5.5	55	6.5	65
	Overall score		71.87		66.38		77.51

(Dark-shaded cells above contain information entered by a box participant; light-shaded cells are computed. Total scores are calculated as weighted averages.)

Note that Ace comes out on top for Jane, given her ratings and her emphasis on ease of learning over features. Apex comes out best for John. When the two perspectives are given equal weight, as here, Apex also comes out as best overall. Were Jane given disproportionate weight—e.g., because she is the senior partner with the largest financial stake in the decision—the result might be different. With an analysis like this in front of them, she and John can productively discuss why they feel differently about which factors are most important or whether some of their ratings of the options should be adjusted.

Acknowledged Limits

Before moving on, let's acknowledge some common reactions to this kind of approach. It may seem both too simplistic and too complex. Too mathematical. Too rational. Misleadingly precise. Where's the emotion? Isn't reality much fuzzier? Do you expect *me* to decide like that?!

Behavioral economists delight in exposing how *ir*rational most decisions are, how seemingly independent factors can influence each other, and how supposedly irrelevant considerations can make a difference. Game theorists remind us of the endless complexity that can emerge as parties to a decision or dispute interact strategically. Choiceboxing does not purport to model all those nuances. It adopts an admittedly "naïve utilitarian" model for the sake of usefulness and usability. Its results are approximate and only as good as the inputs. They are fodder for deliberation and conversation, not definitive pronouncements.

Emotional considerations, by the way, are hardly foreclosed. You can explicitly include "soft" factors like overall impression or gut reaction and weight them as you see fit.

To Box or Not to Box?

Whether to box a choice depends in part on how much effort is required, relative to potential benefit. It's certainly possible that boxing will make some choices harder (even if better).

Knowing when to step back and do a systematic choice analysis is a valuable skill. Here's an approach for judging the threshold suitability of a context for such analysis.

First consider the *characteristics of the choice itself.*

- ♦ Does it involves discrete options among which you need to select?
- ♦ Do the options differ in more than one way that you care about?
- ♦ Can those differences be coherently captured in terms of factors?
- ♦ Is it clear which person's or persons' interests are being measured? Is there a clear time of such measurement? Are there well-defined goals?

Then consider *your needs and circumstances.*

- ♦ What's your relationship to the choice? Are you the decider, a guider, or a provider?
- ♦ What are your goals in terms of wanting to choose carefully? Are you genuinely undecided? Do you need to confirm your decision, document it, or open a fair process around it?
- ♦ What do you know (and need to know)?
  - ♦ You presumably don't yet know whether there may be a clear winner or a clear best choice.
  - ♦ You typically start out with inadequate knowledge in at least one of the dimensions (options, factors, useful alternative perspectives) as well as in the ratings, scoring methods, and weights.
- ♦ Do the benefits of careful deliberation justify the time and other costs involved?
- ♦ Are you prepared to be candid with yourself and others about your real motivations?
- ♦ Are you ready to make this decision? Or are there some preliminary, brush-clearing decisions to be made first? You'll spare yourself frustration by testing and shaping your ideas before going further.

The cost-benefit ratio, of course, is highly dependent on the tools and skills you have available. Specialized software, discussed below, can make systematic decision making much easier. Experience in using it also makes a difference. And if a box is already built for the kind of decision you're facing, the threshold for utilization can be even lower.

Defining Options

For effective choiceboxing, or other systematic deliberation, options should be *simple* and *competitive*. Simple in the sense that each represents a singular thing, not a compound of independently selectable things. Each option should be able to be given a single rating on all potential differentiating factors. Each option should also be competitive in the sense that it is potentially better than at least one other known option on some factor from some perspective that's being taken into account.

Consider casting a wide net. Developing and expanding your range of options is good not only for bargaining leverage but for analytical clarity.

Whatever your method, it's a good practice to record what options you've rejected, and why.

Defining Factors

Factors in turn should be *simple* and *significant*. Simple in the sense that each option can be assigned one and only one rating on each factor. Significant in the sense that each factor makes some option better than another for someone—that it represents a difference someone might care about. You want factors to which you can give a single answer for any option (even if you may be a bit unsure about that answer or others may differ). Each factor should be as distinct and independent as possible.

A good factor is one that captures significant differentiation, either because options vary substantially on it or because it is given great weight. Differentiation will emerge as ratings and weights are expressed and change as options are added and removed. Must-haves and must-not-haves (no-nos) are generally more differentiating than nice-to-haves, but in close cases the latter can be determinative.

Factoring a choice for the first time can be quite challenging. But for repeated choices, the work will repay itself.

Here are steps and questions that will often help factors worth considering surface:

♦ Think of all the ways in which your options are significantly different. What characteristics or consequences make one option better or worse than another?

♦ What differences do you care about? What about others whose perspectives must or should be taken into account?

♦ What do you feel you *should* care about?

♦ Identify the abstract, derivative factors (like "ease of use") that have value consequences even if you can't identify specific features.

- Try to smoke out unspoken factors. Be sure to acknowledge even "bad" reasons that might motivate rationalizations.

- Iterate back and forth between your option list and factor list:
  - What are some things you like about particular options? Why are you leaning toward them?
  - What are some things you dislike about particular options? Why are you hesitating about some? Why are they on the list at all?
  - Why are some options not even on the list?

- Which option do you instinctively like best and least. Why? Are those reasons on your factor list?

- How would the world be different in ways you care about were you to choose a particular option?
  - What positive things would you gain? What would you lose?
  - What negative things would you incur? What would you avoid?

- Ask yourself the "five whys" to get to deep interests and goals. (Each time you answer a question like "Why is this option better?" ask "Why?" in response to the answer.)

- Whenever you catch yourself thinking or talking about a factor that's not on the list, add it.

Keep a record of factors you *considered* including (and why you did or didn't). Record even what you *don't* care about, and why—you or someone else may care about them in a future choice. Preserve, don't discard, your deliberative work product.

Obviously there's little point in actively tracking factors that don't make a difference within the option set you're considering. You don't want to focus on requirements or disqualifications that wouldn't apply to any option actually under consideration. (You might call these "goes without saying" factors.) But keep them around as a checklist against later-added options. Beware of omitting a factor because it doesn't seem to differentiate any current options, only to later add an option that *would* be significantly differentiated on that factor.

Refining Factors

Once you've got a good working factor list, consider whether any are duplicative and can be combined. Consider whether any are compound (not permitting single unambiguous ratings) and need to be split up.

Formulate a succinct prompt or question in terms of which all options can be rated on each factor. They should allow people to unambiguously say which options are better or worse on it.

Ratings should be clearly expressible. People should not have to wonder what a factor means. Ambiguity will show up later as deliberative difficulty.

For each factor, consider the range of possible ratings and define how options should be scored for each such rating. Are there narrowing criteria, like price or feature range thresholds, that would help you focus attention on a smaller set of options? Are any factors so important that a particular rating on them would disqualify an option, regardless of ratings on other factors? Would any rating dispositively *qualify* ("shoe in") an option?

Rating and Weighting

It's a good practice to separate *defining* (options and factors) from *deciding*. Keep an open mind about which options are best and which factors are most important until you've got a decent batch of both on the table.

Factor weights for a given perspective should reflect the participant's opinion about the relative importance of that factor for the person or group *on whose behalf the decision is being made*. Be clear whose interests are being considered.

Focus on major factors (requirements, disqualifications, highly weighted factors) first. Document any assumptions behind your assessments and your weights.

Changes to a factor definition can render prior ratings invalid. It's thus important to settle factors early. Ratings will need at least to be reexamined when a factor or option is redefined.

An inability to say which option is better on a given factor can be due to lack of information, a poorly defined factor, or confusion about the interest perspective from which you are judging. If you find yourself torn between several different ratings for a single cell, you've probably got a compound factor or compound option in your box. If the total scores or rankings seems wrong, there's probably an unarticulated factor or weight differential afoot. You may prefer an option for reasons you hesitate to acknowledge. Try to acknowledge these reasons, even if only to yourself.

Wrapping Up a Choice

Once you've made a choice based on significant deliberation, it's a good practice to make notes for posterity. What options and factors did you consider? How did you rate and weight everything? Were there aspects of your choice that you weren't confident about? What would you tell yourself or others when a similar choice is faced in the future?

After you've acted on a choice, and have had time to experience the results, consider looking back at how it was made. In retrospect, did you miss any important factors or grant some inappropriate weight? Did you neglect to consider options that might have changed the result? What would you do differently were you to face such a choice again?

Group Choosing

In both personal and business settings, many choices involve groups of people. The choiceboxing methods are especially useful for group decision making. Each person can have his or her own perspective layer and make independent assessments both of how options compare on factors and how the factors compare in terms of importance.

Objectives can be in conflict, in that they are not mutually achievable. Satisfying one may mean not satisfying another. People's opinions about the *importance* of objectives will also typically vary. Trade-offs of both goals and perspectives are often inescapable.

Encourage people to work independently on their perspectives, not reviewing each other's ratings and weights until they are provisionally finished. Doing so will help to avoid groupthink.

Keep in mind that people often don't have fixed preferences. Interactions with others can change how we view what we want or think is best. Most of us are open to persuasion and willing to listen to the views and needs of friends and colleagues.

Once a group box has been constructed and populated, lots of useful discussion topics suggest themselves. Points of consensus can be noted. Areas of disagreement can be highlighted. People can suggest that their colleagues explain or reconsider ratings or weights.

Governance of a box's structure is best *not* left to the group. Generally, only one person should have the power to delete or change the definition of options or factors. That should ideally happen before ratings begin in earnest. But *adding* options and factors can be done without much hesitation, since participants always have the ability to set weights to zero or decline to rate certain options on certain factors.

While perspective layers are most often found in group decision-making contexts, such layers can be used to approach a decision from alternative points of view even by a single decision maker.

Multiple perspectives will often enhance the quality of a decision. One person's ratings may be premised on factual errors, wrong assumptions, or misunderstandings. Independent assessments are useful to smoke them out.

Risk and Uncertainty

Choiceboxing is most useful when you are uncertain about which options get you the most net benefit and you can't easily balance the trade-offs involved. It doesn't offer any special advantages when your uncertainty is about what will *happen*. Decision-analysis software like TreeAge Pro (**http://www.treeage.com**) is far better suited for those kinds of decisions, especially when the possible outcomes have their own further uncertainties. By assigning values and probabilities to branches of a decision tree, you can gain insights into what strategies are likely to yield the best results.

The relative risks and potential upsides of options can, however, be at least roughly captured as factors in a choicebox. You can add comments to ratings and weights to signal uncertainty or lack of confidence. If uncertainty applies to an entire factor (i.e., it won't make a difference if certain circumstances arise), you can discount it appropriately by adjusting the weight.

Beyond Choice

There are good uses for structured approaches to choices beyond choice itself. Once you have a solid framework for approaching the assessments and tradeoffs involved in a choice situation, you can use it as an instrument for understanding yourself and others better. Boxing can surface unarticulated expectations and educate your instincts.

You can engage in "shadowboxing" by anticipating the preferences of opponents, counterparties, or decision makers. Put yourself in their shoes and draft a set of ratings and weights that likely represents their perspective. What do they care most and least about? Where are their views most different from your own? If they seem to assess an option inadequately or disproportionately on certain factors, how might you influence them to change?

When it comes to negotiation, understanding the different preference profiles of the parties will sometimes yield win-win solutions you might otherwise miss. Think of labor and management conflicts, for instance. One party can frame its positions and arguments in terms that address the likely motivating concerns of the other.

Consider how you might use a choicebox in advising a client. By laying out the considerations and judgments behind your advice, or jointly working through them, communication can be improved. The client might draw your attention to factors you've neglected or help uncover mistaken assumptions. Some firms might even want to consider placing choiceboxes on their extranets for clients to use in handling routine operational decisions that have legal repercussions.

The Value-add of Choice-making Tools

Choiceboxing can be done in principle with little more technology than a pencil and paper. (Nontrivial choices worth boxing present too many options, factors, and trade-offs to keep reliably in your head.) But choiceboxing is not practical without better tools. Scoring functions and related bookkeeping cry out for software.

You can perform basic weighted factor analysis using Word tables and functions. Choiceboxes can be implemented as three-dimensional spreadsheets in applications like Microsoft Excel (using multiple sheets and lots of tricky formulas).

But specialized software is required to realize the full potential of choiceboxing. Such software can make it easy to reconfigure options and factors, perform useful analytics, and document your decisions. There are sophisticated (and expensive) applications that are best suited for experts and also modestly priced desktop tools that you can find by Googling "decision support software." Some colleagues and I have developed a system that is optimized for collaborative deliberation over the Internet.

Visit this book's companion Web site to learn more (**www.SmarterLegal Work.com**).

Having choices is the essence of freedom. Choosing well is the essence of responsibility. Knowledge tools can help you choose both more freely *and* more responsibly.

Going Deeper

Gilbert, Daniel, *Stumbling on Happiness,* New York: Vintage Books, 2006.

Hammond, John S., Ralph L. Keeney, and Howard Raiffa, *Smart Choices,* New York: Broadway Books, 1999.

Klein, Gary, *Intuition at Work,* New York: Doubleday, 2003.

Lehrer, Jonah, *How We Decide,* New York: Mariner Books, 2009.

Kopeikina, Luda, *The Right Decision Every Time*, Upper Saddle River, New Jersey: Prentice Hall, 2005.

Luce, R. Duncan, and Howard Raiffa, *Games and Decisions*, 1967.

Nagel, Stuart S., *Using Personal Computers for Decision-Making in Law Practice,* 1985.

Schwartz, Barry, *The Paradox of Choice*, New York: HarperCollins Publishers, Inc., 2004.

Underhill, Paco, *Why We Buy*, New York: Simon & Schuster, 1999.

CHAPTER FIFTEEN

Other Tools

I'VE COVERED THE MAJOR categories of legal knowledge tools, but plenty of others remain, and new ones will continue to be invented. There are "been there, done that" systems (experiential databases), knowledge portals, and taxonomy engines. There are all kinds of visualization tools that provide powerful ways to represent and manipulate legal information.

For example, IPVision (**http://ipvisioninc.com**) provides stunning visualizations of patent portfolios and surrounding intellectual property landscapes. In the area of contracts and similar legal documents, Kiiac (**http://www.kiiac.com/**) uses graphics and colors to communicate analytical insights gained by applying advanced statistical techniques to collections of texts.

One category worth special mention is *computer-aided instruction and e-learning*. Many readers will be familiar with offerings from the Center for Computer-Assisted Legal Instruction (CALI). Its interactive lessons on topics of legal substance and procedure perform many knowledge tool functions, in terms of embodying and facilitating intelligence. Similar materials are available from continuing legal education providers and commercial publishers.

In addition to using such tools to educate themselves, some innovative lawyers and service providers are using e-learning techniques to educate clients. Online instruction systems in areas like sexual harassment and regulatory compliance can be powerful—and profitable—ways to deliver valuable service.

Going Deeper

SubTech (short for International Conference on Substantive Technology in Law Practice and Legal Education) is an invitational event that has happened every two years since 1990. See **http://legaltechcenter.net/subtech/** for information about the 2008 conference at William & Mary Law School. The 2010 one will be in Zaragoza, Spain. If you are actively involved in both legal education and substantive technology, you should consider getting involved.

Interlude

Knowledge Wasteland

Working Dumb in an Age of Smart Machines

Ask yourself these questions:

- Do you leave your faucets running at home while you're at work?
- Do you turn outside floodlights on during the daytime?
- Do you leave your car idling in the parking lot while shopping?
- Do you use your main oven to toast a bagel?
- Do you throw away your dishes and silverware after a meal? Toss books after you've read them?

No? How about these:

- Do you mow your lawn with hand scissors?
- Do you calculate complex budgets with pencil and paper?
- When you put on that home addition, did you use toothpicks instead of two-by-fours?

Most of us don't intentionally do those kinds of things. Even though modern societies tolerate a lot of waste, certain practices just seem to cross our threshold of unacceptability. We're wasteful but also selectively waste averse. Most of us especially hate to have our time wasted and have a sense of environmental responsibility (so long as it is not *too* inconvenient). We react immediately to the above examples because, in the first group, valuable resources (water, electricity, gas, cutlery) are being consumed for no good reason and, in the second category, human time and energy are.

What does this have to do with lawyers?

More than we care to admit, I'm afraid.

As a practitioner, teacher of practitioners, and maker of software tools for practitioners, I've seen more lawyers in more practice contexts than most. Training and consulting work takes me behind the scenes in many different legal work settings.

My honest impression is that practices as laughably wasteful as those above occur just about *every* day in *every* law practice in the country. I'm not talking about all the paper we recklessly proliferate or the untouched luncheon sandwiches that get trashed while homeless folks beg for food downstairs. I'm talking about our core professional activities. In an age of intelligent technology and "working smart," too many of us work dumb. We constantly redo, reinvent, forget, misremember, misplace.

You might say that we lawyers live in a knowledge wasteland.

Knowledge Mismanagement

Law is arguably among the most wasteful of the professions: one thinks first of people- and paper-intensive discovery battles and mega-trials, but resource extravagance pervades many practices. Lawyers' professional zeal and pride are not always compatible with a philosophy of conservation. We are especially susceptible to "not invented here" and "hey, the client isn't complaining" rationales.

Few firms have successfully implemented comprehensive in-house brief banks or expert systems yet, and significant amounts of legal research, document drafting, and transaction planning are needlessly redone throughout the bar for lack of systematic means of recovering prior work product.

Part of the transformative potential of information technology is the opportunity it affords to apply lawyering expertise to the practice itself. Design skills routinely used in the construction of documents, deals, arguments, and organizations can be redirected to the lawyering work process.

The Price We Pay

Many lawyers lead lives of quiet desperation. Work is made up of long stretches of boredom and drudgery, punctuated by periods of frantic activity, and only occasionally of "flow" (that blissful state of full engagement in a work task documented by Mihaly Csikszentmihalyi.[1])

Wastefulness imposes many kinds of penalties:

- ◆ Long hours
- ◆ Mindless repetition
- ◆ Stress
- ◆ Lost profits
- ◆ Unsatisfactory results

The effective use of knowledge is more than just effective *time* management, more than effective *document* management, more than effective *case* management. It's a pervasive matter of getting optimal returns on intellectual effort.

Knowledge systems, then, are important adjuncts to time-management and personal-effectiveness techniques.

Waste Not, Want Not

Most lawyers work far less effectively than they recognize or acknowledge. In the context of modern tools and methods, some of our practices are downright stupid. What a waste!

The fact is that much of what lawyers continue to do "by hand" (and "by head") is much better done by machine. Those who understand that shouldn't apologize for pointing it out. Only a very small percentage of what can appropriately and cost-effectively be done by our nonbiological assistants is so done.

I've heard it said that "lawyers who *can* be replaced by computers, *should* be." (In other words, if you're no better than a machine, maybe you belong in a different line of work.) Few if any should or will be replaced anytime soon. But we will see an accelerating trend toward the delegation of routine knowledge tasks to machines. Many lawyering tasks can and should be automated. And those lawyers who persist in wasting effort on mechanical tasks will deserve little sympathy as circumstances turn against them.

---

[1] Csikszentmihalyi, Mihaly, *Flow: The Psychology of Optimal Experience,* New York: Harper and Row Publishers, 1991.

I count myself among those who believe the world needs *more* lawyering—effectively done, appropriately delivered, fairly distributed. Despite our inefficiencies, most lawyers do a lot of good work, and many live happy and prosperous lives. Just think how much better things could be if we weren't quite so wasteful.

PART THREE

Why

To PROPERLY EVALUATE KNOWLEDGE tools, you've got to take a very broad view of both benefits and costs. We tend not to think broadly enough about either of them. People focus on a few key benefits and then a few key costs. If it just so happens that the costs they've identified are less than the benefits, they feel they've made their case. That's like comparing two icebergs based on the shapes that happen to loom above the waterline from a particular angle. How can we manage our tools and uses so that we do achieve a significant net benefit over the potential costs and downsides?

In this section, we'll consider benefits, costs, motivations, and inhibitions.

CHAPTER SIXTEEN

Benefits

WHAT'S THE POINT OF all this? Why would we want to use knowledge tools in law practice? What benefits do these technologies offer? Here are common answers.

Productivity (Efficiency)

The classic benefit of knowledge tools is more efficient production of work. By enlisting them, you can generate more work product in less time, with less investment of current intellectual effort.

Streamlining practice promises more productivity, less waste. Efficiency is promoted by systems that spare us from giving information more than once, giving information that is not needed, and making decisions that mechanically flow from known circumstances.

Suppose you model a complex document, like a complex will or trust. You capture regularities such as what paragraphs go where under what circumstances, what sections need to be added if a client lives in a certain jurisdiction, what issues are presented by a certain configuration of facts. By doing this, you can often take a process that takes people dozen of hours to perform and produce documents that are just as good if not better, with only an hour or less of a human's time.

It's Monday morning. You're a midlevel associate at a large firm, coffee in hand, about to settle into work after a rare weekend of relaxation. A fax is sitting on your chair. It seems that the town of Wellville has finally decided to float that bond for the new school building. Market conditions are such that time is of the essence. Several hundred pages of documents may need to be completed. A few days' delay could cost the town tens of thousands of dollars if interest rates rise as many predict. Missing sections or inappropriate phrases could spell embarrassment at best and costly malpractice at worst.

Last year, these kinds of transactions typically took a small team of lawyers, paralegals, and secretaries two days of feverish work. Examples were found of similar transactions in the firm's document collection and copied into a new draft. Then the parts that obviously didn't apply were deleted, and parts that were obviously missing, but needed for the peculiarities of the current deal, were found in yet other old documents. Names were adjusted by global search and replace. Dates and numbers were individually edited to reflect the terms of the current deal. Everything was proofed and then sent to the associate in charge, who still found dozens of little errors and inappropriate and missing passages. This cycle continued a few times, until the documents were sent for "final" review by the partner, who might discover a major inconsistency between two sections, requiring yet another round of editing and proofing. After nearly thirty-six hours, a finished package could be sent to the client, who not uncommonly would decide to change a few details at the last minute to reflect negotiations with the funding bank.

This year, fortunately, the firm's new automated practice system for municipal finance documents is in place. You enter details from the term sheet faxed by the client on a series of screens that adjust to present only those questions that must be answered for the situation described. All the basic legal and strategic choices needed to draft documents are presented for your point-and-shoot disposition. Since this is a kind of transaction the system has been programmed to handle, you quickly review your answers, click a button, and smile as 120 pages of customized documents appear on the screen. You're confident that 95% of the grunt work has been done and that the drafts will contain few if any of the picky little mistakes so common last year. And if the client needs a change at the last minute, you know you can accommodate it without panic. The coffee is still warm . . .

Responsiveness (Quick Turnaround)

In addition to efficient use of human resources, speed of production also enables rapid turnaround—a distinct value of systematization. Being able to get things done in less elapsed time sometimes is more important than how efficiently you get them done. There can be phenomenal advantages to speed of production. Rapid response is often of high strategic value to a client. Getting solid legal work done fast is sometimes espoused as the foremost rationale for practice systems.

In this way, efficient systems can help produce *outstanding* service, service that exceeds expectations and delights the client.

It's late Friday afternoon. You're a legal services lawyer in an urban office. This week you've interviewed eight new clients, deposed a witness, handled three hearings, and gone through six hours of bitter negotiation with a landlord and his lawyer. You've worked late into the evening several days, as usual.

Your secretary appears in the door frame: "I gotta go; the kids are waiting. Have a good weekend. Oh, by the way, Abigail Smith is here. Looks like she got that eviction notice after all."

Abigail is a longstanding client with the annoying habit of showing up with important papers right before the deadline for responding to them. You sigh, look at your tickets for the baseball game that begins in two hours, and say, "All right, send her in." Abigail shows you the complaint and summons she got last week. You know that an answer is due Monday, and Monday you're supposed to be at the other end of the state doing training. But you also remember that your assembly system for eviction defense documents will make quick work of your responsive paperwork. Since you already know the essential facts of this case well, if you're lucky you can persuade Abigail not to tell you too much about her new cat, crank out a perfect set of defenses, interrogatories and the like, along with a cover letter to the clerk, and drop them in the mailbox on the way to the game . . .

Quality of Work (Accuracy, Thoroughness)

Quality improvement is another distinct benefit. By capturing carefully designed and time-tested documents and methods in systems, lawyers can achieve a higher quality of work product—both in terms of legal correctness and strategic optimality. Systems can reduce missed deadlines, formalities, issues, and arguments. Because computers virtually never make logical or mathematical errors, they can promote the systematic consideration of alternatives, articulation of goals, and planning of means that excellent law practice presupposes.

Properly designed and used, knowledge systems improve not only efficiency but also quality. They assist in producing work that's free of error and is valid and complete.

Systems can help make sure that everything is done that needs to be done, that all of the important issues have been dealt with. They can step you through a well-structured analytical problem, present you with decisions you need to make, and, based on your answers and your inputs, produce a document—or an analysis or a recommended set of actions. They can advise you on what positions to take and what forms you need to file.

> It's Christmas Eve. Horace Witherspoon is unexpectedly in the waiting room. It seems that he and his wife are off to Venice for the holidays, and he's picked this time to make a long-planned revision to his will. It involves a complicated restructuring of the trusts into which most of the estate pours. Your efforts to discourage his last-minute revisions are unavailing.
>
> Ordinarily you would be uncomfortable drafting the necessary instruments and having them executed without careful proofreading and a colleague's review. But your estate-planning system has been in regular use for several years now and routinely produces flawless documents, now that a dozen lawyers have used it extensively and participated in its refinement. You bring up Horace's previous information, specify the desired changes, and assemble the needed paperwork. An alert reminds you to check an obscure possibility that turns out not to be problematic. Two late-working staff members serve as witnesses. The Witherspoons are on their way, and so are you . . .

Consistency

A body of work can exhibit high quality and accuracy but lack consistency in content or style. Knowledge systems can help you maintain standards of consistency. In corporate settings, customer and partner experiences are enhanced when similar transactions are handled with similar documents regardless of the lawyer who happens to work on them.

Knowledge tools enable lawyers to work more consistently on a conceptual level in their cases, with less required attention to mechanical details. As one can modify parts of word-processed documents with confidence that new errors have not been introduced into other parts, it is possible to modify certain facts, choices, or judgments in a practice system "answer file" with confidence that legally appropriate changes are made where needed to keep the proffered advice and documents valid. You can choose to assert a particular claim in a complaint and count on the system to prompt for necessary new information, warn about possible inconsistencies or duplications, and formulate appropriate language.

Quality of Work Life (Job Satisfaction)

Greater job satisfaction is yet another reason for system development and use. Most lawyers are happier and more productive when spared the mechanical tedium of much "legal" work. We prefer not to have to write each pro forma letter to the client accompanying recently received interrogatories or manually insert a counterclaim that always flows from a certain defense in a particular kind of action. We'd rather have computers take care of such details as making sure that pronouns and verbs are of the appropriate gender and number, that paragraphs are sequentially numbered, that cross-references get updated when a document changes, and that punctuation and pagination come out right.

There's more to life than work, and more to work than productivity. You ought to be able to express yourself in your work, to contribute your individuality and creativity. Professional practice is a craft we should be able to take pride in, get satisfaction from. It should produce a sense of well-being. People are happier if they work in a way that produces quality results with less drudgery.

Knowledge systems can give us more control, more self-determination. By offloading routine, mechanical work to machines, where it belongs, these systems can be a humanizing force. They offer at least some relief from the tyranny of the billable hour, some prospect of capitalizing knowledge in systems that yield value even when we are not personally turning the crank.

Building and using knowledge systems can also result in more collegiality. I've seen systems that generate team sprit by having people work together to maintain them. The system becomes an object of group pride and a tool for expressing the members' collective knowledge.

Good knowledge systems can also give you permission to forget. Some of us need to cultivate the skill of forgetting gracefully.

Practice Improvement

Systematizing and formalizing practical lawyering knowledge is a prerequisite to embedding it effectively in a computer program. This requirement can have the benevolent effect of forcing a reexamination of how work is actually being done and might be improved.

In working with law offices to build systems, I often find that people discover things they've been missing. They realize they've embodied and systematized rules that are no longer valid. Two experts will sit down and talk about it: "You've been doing what?!" and "I can't believe that we've never seen this problem that's been systematically present in our practice." The job of automating practice can itself serve as a way to enrich the practice through improvement. System work supplies opportunities for cross-correlation of expertise, creative redesign, and novel strategies. It can reveal questionable practices that are ordinarily submerged in murky depths.

Reduced Reliance on Scarce Experts

As noted in Chapter 10, human experts are often too busy for routine consultation, and may become unavailable for any number of reasons. When aspects of their expertise are embodied in a knowledge system, it can be drawn upon at any time.

In the longer term, substantive systems can serve as part of an office's institutional memory. They can be viewed as knowledge assets that allow certain kinds of expertise to be made available at more times and to more people than that of a human expert and insulate an organization somewhat from the temporary or permanent absence of especially knowledgeable staff. Know-how can thus be leveraged and preserved as an accreting repository for collective use.

Training and Continuing Education

Systems can be used to educate users about substance and procedure as issues are encountered in a work process. People can learn at their own pace and "just in time."

Systems can also provide guidance in situations where people may be reluctant to talk with other people—e.g., to explain delicate aspects of office policy or advise on troublesome ethical issues.

But what about the famous "McDonaldization" of legal practice—the concern that, "Gee, if it just becomes a matter of filling in the facts and pushing a button, and out pops the will, how are associates going to learn?" It's a refrain I often hear. People say, "I don't want to use any of this document-assembly stuff," or "I don't want to use these practice systems," because they produce unthinking practitioners. My response is usually something like this: "It's always a matter of how you implement and the decisions you make about how to build these technologies. These dangers are not inherent. The technology itself is unbiased on that question. Systems can be built that can enhance knowledge, that can enhance learning, and that can produce people who think more and think more creatively through the process just as they can be written to stifle creativity and reduce knowledge."

The empowerment that flows from knowledge tools brings reliance as well, and one possible effect is the atrophy of certain lawyering competencies—as electronic calculators have reduced our skills at doing math in our heads or on paper. We may find it difficult or impossible to practice law without computational assistants.

Marketing and Recruitment Advantages

As discussed in Chapter 10 with respect to document assembly, advanced knowledge tools can be showcased for purposes of marketing your services and recruiting colleagues. Clients increasingly encounter such tools in their own businesses, and prefer to engage professionals who demonstrate appropriate technological proficiency. Systems that make the client experience more satisfying and cost effective will give you an edge over less savvy competitors.

Similarly, lawyers and other personnel naturally gravitate to law offices that provide work environments in which they can shine. Intelligent systems that foster and reward human creativity are becoming essential parts of the legal work place. They can help you recruit and retain top candidates.

More Flexible Allocation of Work

Systems often offer opportunities to restructure the allocation of legal work across the various players in the office. They can both transform the role of support staff, and increase the delegability of work.

Certain kinds of knowledge systems can result in a law office requiring less time of nonbillable people, lowering overhead. These technologies enable attorneys to do work themselves more efficiently that may previously have required support staff, who probably did things they didn't find very satisfying anyway, like cataloging documents or generating routine forms.

At the same time, these systems can help you delegate work. You can pass work to people who might previously not have been able to handle it but can now by virtue of having knowledge tools in place. You may be able to delegate work to secretaries, paralegals, or associates or law student interns who might otherwise not effectively handle it.

Second-Order Benefits

All of the above benefits can flow directly from the successful implementation of legal knowledge systems. Many of these benefits in turn lay the groundwork for other, more general, desirable results. How those play out will depend on the broader organizational and financial health of the firm. Great strides in efficiency, responsiveness, and marketability may trigger dramatically increased profitability in one office, while merely enabling another to survive or remain competitive.

CHAPTER SEVENTEEN

Costs

LET'S JUMP TO COSTS, downsides, disadvantages, and dangers. What goes on the other side of the ledger? What price might you have to pay for all the wonderful benefits recounted in the last chapter?

If you're a typical lawyer, you can't help but to have been thinking about the negatives while reading the last chapter. (That's what we do.)

It's important at the outset to distinguish the following:

- *Upfront* costs from *ongoing* costs
- The costs of *building* tools from those of *buying* prebuilt ones
- The costs when things go *right* from those when things go *wrong*

As you might expect, start-up costs for knowledge tools typically represent a bigger fiscal bump than ongoing costs, custom software development can introduce major new categories of expense, and everything is better when things go right!

When You Buy

Application Software Licenses
The most immediate cost when you purchase a prepackaged knowledge tool is the software license itself. Packages typically range from a few hundred dollars to a few thousand dollars per seat. Sometimes this price is repeated in the form of an annual subscription; generally there is a smaller annual maintenance charge. And periodically you will face a more substantial charge for a major revision or upgrade.

"Software as a Service" (SaaS) arrangements, not discussed here, are beginning to change the economics of knowledge tool utilization by letting you "rent" rather than buy needed tools.

Infrastructure Costs

Most knowledge tools sit on top of existing technology infrastructure. In other words, you don't usually need to buy new computers or operating software. But sometimes you will need to incur system integration costs to make these tools behave well with your other systems. For example, you may need to migrate to a new version of Microsoft Office.

Time

The biggest cost factor typically is *time*—time of partners, associates, paralegals, secretaries, technical staff, and managers. Time that is either diverted from fee-generating work, in the case of time-keepers, or from other useful and productive activities, in the case of staff members. Here are some of the activities you need to anticipate:

- ♦ Finding and choosing the right packages
- ♦ Training and learning (both giving and getting)
- ♦ Support for users

When You Build

Engine and Tool-Making Tool Licenses

When you *build* knowledge tools (either starting from scratch or doing major customization), you typically pay a license fee for "platform" or "engine" software. Rather than buying tools with prefabricated content, you're buying tools for making tools. Sometimes these only need to be licensed for those doing actual development; other times, each user of the ultimate application needs to have a license.

But once again, the largest cost is time. Let's look at the major categories of personnel cost associated with building knowledge systems.

Legal Professional Time

Nonbillable professional time is usually by far the most significant cost factor. If you're building a knowledge system of any sort, you need a knowledgeable person. Often the most knowledgeable and useful people for input to these systems are expensive and busy. Sometimes you've got to take people who the office can least afford off the production line and dedicate their attention to ramping up production capacity.

Technical Staff Time

If you in-source the software development, you will dedicate your own staff time to activities like planning and analysis, coding, testing, rollout, and integration. They will likely also need time to get up to speed on the platform being used.

Ongoing *maintenance* of applications is often overlooked. Technology keeps shifting, as do the practice contexts it supports. It takes vigilance and effort to keep systems working well. Knowledge systems can be especially fragile, and even short periods of inattention can make them disproportionately less useful.

Management Time

Knowledge system projects can require quite a bit of attention from managers and administrators. You've got to motivate people, you've got to track them, and you've got to worry about how this stuff fits in with the technology environment generally, the staffing and the consulting contracts that are necessary to pull them off, and the billing innovations that might be necessary to take advantage of them. So there can be a lot of management overhead.

Consultant and Contractor Fees

When you bring in outsiders to help, as developers, trainers, or mentors, their fees can be substantial. Some of these folks charge lawyer rates.

When Things Go Wrong

Even in the best circumstances, there are transitional inefficiencies and distractions in moving away from your antecedent systems. You will fail to anticipate costs and consequences and learn from experience. But plans can go awry in more serious ways, and no project should be commenced without at least considering the dangers.

One way to identify other possible costs is to think about benefits outlined in the last chapter and imagine their dark sides, their evil twins. It's important to acknowledge that there are counter-examples for all of the wonderful positives of knowledge tools.

For example, time and money spent building and maintaining unduly complicated or poorly designed systems can *reduce* overall productivity. Similarly, systems can promote *bad* practice by having incomplete, outdated, or otherwise inaccurate "knowledge" programmed into them. Indeed, the supposed infallibility of the machine can make such defects especially pernicious.

Poorly implemented systems can produce sloppy law by encouraging a sense of complacency. The real challenge is to design, use, and train people to use these power tools responsibly. You can't let people off the hook: they're still professionally responsible for their work product. People need to invest in authorship—not only in the output but in the system itself. They should contribute to the systems so that good law gets practiced systematically as opposed to episodically.

Systematization has the potential to stifle creativity, routinize practice, and dehumanize the workplace. Formulation of practice protocols and standards in the narrow terms a computer can manipulate poses dangers of overreliance on the quantifiable and logical, to the detriment of more "fuzzy" human considerations. There can be virtues in disorganization and serendipity. Sometimes a reinvented wheel is better.

We need to be aware, when we talk about the virtues of consistency, of the downsides and problems and the concomitant value of originality and creativity. Systems should be designed and managed in ways that promote consistency within the limited spaces where consistency is really important and that's what the client wants, not to steamroll our creative ideas that may be the very things clients need. You need to ask, "Am I stifling creativity? Am I ruling out originality? Am I reducing quality by trying to achieve efficiency?"

In pursuing the many undoubted benefits of practice systematization, one must be alert to these hazards. The legal workplace is an immensely complex system in its own right, and technological interventions can have unforeseen consequences. Although our modern tools can assist us as reminders, organizers, quality controllers, issue spotters, and coaches, they can't compensate for low practice standards or poor work habits. At best, they are people enhancers. It is up to us to use them well.

There are also all-too-common risks of non-completion, nonuse, abandonment, obsolescence, and irrelevance to developing practice.

It's important to stress that the goal is more and better communication among people, not less. But even collegiality can have a dark side. People can get in each others' ways when asked to come up with the best ways of doing something. There are many opportunities for collision. I've seen experts disagree violently about whether to have a tab after the period or a space, whether the footnotes are centered on the bottom of the page, or whether to put a comma before the conjunction in a series.

Perhaps if we make the work too easy, with too many power tools, people will find it less satisfying. Although I challenge you to find a carpenter who says, "You know, I really prefer cutting boards by hand. I get a thrill out of sawing two-by-fours." If there's a power tool, they'll use the power tool to do that job and go on to the more craftsman-like aspects of carpentry.

CHAPTER EIGHTEEN

The Balancing Act

SUPPOSE THAT SOMEONE YOU trust offered you a set of tools or methods that enabled you to do work of higher quality in less time. In exchange for some of your time and money now, you would gain several multiples of that investment over the next year, and the year after that, and the year after that. Would you do it? Naturally, you would want to ask questions: "What exactly are you proposing? What are the costs and risks? How real and likely are the benefits? Why should I believe you?" ("And by the way, where were you ten years ago?")

We're constantly trading off present pain for future gain each time we do an implicit calculus, a mini-return on investment (ROI) analysis. All things considered, are we likely to be better off going one way or the other? We make calculated gambles.

When it comes to bigger questions, like whether to buy a suite of specialized software for a practice group or embark on a knowledge tool development project, one feels the need to be a little more systematic.

The basic questions, from a bean-counter point of view, are these: Is the present value of the benefits, discounted by their probability of not occurring, greater than the present value of the probable costs? And is it *sufficiently* greater to justify the opportunity costs of foregoing alternative investments of time and money? Our inner accountants talk in terms of value propositions, returns on investment, and payback periods.

Difficulties of Quantification

It is rare that you can satisfactorily quantify the specific costs and benefits involved in a significant organizational or technological change. ROI complexities are generic to almost any law office decision—shall we move our office? recarpet? promote someone to partner? open a new office? upgrade to Windows 7?

Knowledge systems aren't much different.

Part of the problem is the inherent intangibility of the assets being acquired or constructed. Economists talk about new means of measuring wealth, and at some point firms and other organizations will track the ebbs and flows of intellectual capital in their accounting systems. We're not there yet.

And there can be great uncertainties about the fact, the size, and the timing of the potential costs and benefits. We need to deal in likelihoods—not only whether, but when, and of what magnitude. Every new technology, like every change, has unforeseen and unintended consequences. Many of these factors are beyond your control. For example, will key people stay? Will demand for this service continue? The situation on which you base your cost/benefit analysis, of course, is also changing as you implement, sometimes in reaction to that very activity. There can be unpredictable interactions with other initiatives and events.

You can imagine plotting benefit and cost streams across the time dimension. (See the graph below, with costs as the dark line and benefits as the light one.) A more accurate portrayal would show these as cloud-like probability distributions.

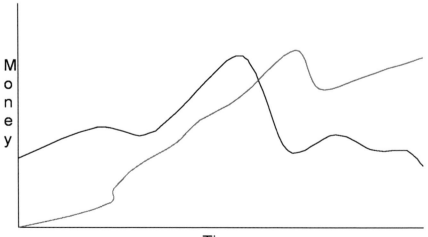

Money

Time

Even in retrospect, there are always issues of attribution. Which actions actually caused which benefits/costs? Interdependencies are rampant. For example, was it really our fancy new document assembly system that won us the Mega Enterprises account, or was it the hypnotic personality of our lead partner?

A related problem is that of allocation—benefits and costs will fall unevenly on the various stakeholders. A benefit to one stakeholder may be a cost to another. Costs and benefits are not neutrally shared across an organization. The distorted incentives produced by such imbalances are considered in the next chapter.

A Practical Process

All this being said, the net benefits of knowledge tools are often obvious and clearly felt. Don't fall victim to paralysis by analysis. Here are practical suggestions for managing the decision process.

The most common problem I see is people being too selective in their thinking. They are inattentive to the full costs, and the full benefits, of knowledge tool initiatives. You need to cast a wide net and use a wide-angle lens. Think of full system cost—the "total cost of ownership." Don't be blindsided by unanticipated expenses. But also don't prematurely discard a promising project out of failure to recognize non-obvious benefits.

I often use the metaphor of two icebergs. Most of their bulk, of course, lies beneath the surface, out of view. But their surface shapes from particular angles may mislead you as to which is really bigger. You need to look closely at both the benefit berg and the cost berg.

Even if you can't realistically quantify all the costs and benefits, it is still essential to *identify* the components. Once they are on the table it is usually possible to make rough but confident inequalities—like the bundle of costs X, Y, and Z is less than the bundle of benefits A, B, and C. Make your assumptions explicit. Record and review them. (Smart choice making is addressed in Chapter 14.)

Not every candidate purchase or project justifies extended analysis. It's useful to have a threshold test. I recommend a simple three-pronged test for judging the suitability of a knowledge technology initiative:

- ◆ Can the proposed technology significantly improve the work in question?
- ◆ Is that work especially valuable or strategic to the organization?
- ◆ Is there a good degree of participant enthusiasm, access, and availability?

The first test is often passed quickly. But the second two require sober reflection. Even an initiative with extraordinary theoretical cost/benefit justification is rarely worth embarking on if it lacks strategic priority and enthusiastic stakeholders.

Don't forget to recalibrate as a project proceeds and as the business and technical contexts evolve.

Are You Prepared to Profit?

The benefits of knowledge system initiatives, of course, depend sharply on how they are implemented. Will you make good choices along the way? Can you assume competent management and rollout?

Harvesting full value from these investments may require significant revisions in how you do business. If you are not prepared for that, such investments may not be for you. On the other hand, you may not be long for survival in law practice, either.

One key issue is that of billing practices. If you continue to bill by the hour for services that now require significantly less lawyer time due to technology investments, you're going to lose, not gain, money. In many situations, it is necessary to implement alternative billing approaches to get maximal returns on investments. This is discussed in detail in Chapter 22.

Do you have, or are you prepared to establish, billing practices that will enable you to reap the harvest of your knowledge system investments? Do you have, or are you prepared to establish, reward structures that will motivate partners and staff to contribute to and use these systems?

CHAPTER NINETEEN

Inhibitions and Motivations

HOWEVER WONDERFUL KNOWLEDGE TOOLS might sound, the reality is that few lawyers are clamoring for them. Why? What are the obstacles to law office adoption?

It has long been utterly clear to me that knowledge technology can radically improve the lives of lawyers and clients. Properly applied, its benefits can dwarf its costs. I hope by now that you agree this is true in at least some circumstances. But I've also come to appreciate how deeply counter it is to many of our practices, arrangements, and attitudes.

Why don't more lawyers use knowledge tools? What's stopping them? Who *wouldn't* want to get better work done in less time for more money and happier clients?

I'm afraid that this is like asking questions like, "Why do people overeat and under-exercise?" or "Why do lawyers under-delegate and under-market?" We routinely fail to do many things that are "good for us." They often require inputs that are in short supply, like faith, effort, discipline, and trust.

I've encountered lots of obstacles and inhibitions to knowledge tool adoption in my years as a practice systems evangelist, and collecting them has become a bit of a hobby. Below are the common ones I've identified. Some of these barriers only apply to private law firms, or only to larger offices. And some only apply to specific stages of knowledge technology, such as building, using, financing, starting, or sustaining. But they are all worth acknowledging. If you know of other good ones, please let me know!

Explanations vs. Excuses

For the most part, lawyers are not stupider or lazier than the average human—there are good reasons why some have not yet adopted this technology. You can be motivated by a rational comparison of costs and benefits and reach a position on the merits. You might honestly conclude that knowledge tools are of too limited applicability to your practice or are too costly or risky. You may feel that the net gain is not that clear. You may have competing investments with higher returns, better things to which to devote organizational energy and scarce funds.

Resistance can be legitimate, even if not narrowly rational. The perceived advantage might not be substantial. "That doesn't seem much better than what I'm doing now." Or you may say, "I'd just rather not do this." Or maybe you accurately perceive your inability or unwillingness to use knowledge tools effectively. It's foolish to pay for membership in a fitness club you won't visit.

But there are also lots of bad reasons.

Too Busy Bailing

A fundamental reality is that many legal professionals find themselves "too busy bailing to patch the hole in the boat." Or, to change metaphors, we're so busy cutting, we don't have time to sharpen the saw. Or yet again, we're too busy driving to stop for gas.

People don't feel they have spare time to ramp up, let alone to ramp up for ramping up.

This may be due to pressure to meet billable hour quotas, concern to meet client demands, or a sense of needing to get while the getting's good.

Part of this is the triumph of the urgent over the important. Many lawyers are urgency addicts. This greases the way for procrastination: "It'll be cheaper next year." And knowledge tools by definition are not things you can build or buy at the last minute, producing the "It's quicker to do it myself" reaction.

People in law offices seem to have especially limited attention and bandwidth for things out of the ordinary. You might call it a mindshare famine.

Instant gratification is the general message of our culture, media, and advertising. This obsession with the present hinders future-oriented projects like knowledge codification. Things that require deferred gratification and un-maximized current income get short shrift.

Ch-Ch-Ch-Changes

If you wear a watch, humor me for a moment and put it on the opposite wrist. (If not, relocate your wallet or a piece of jewelry.)

Change is constant, but it's often unpleasant. It takes us out of the comfort zone. We have an innate resistance to change, as humans. We stick to routines in most precincts of our lives. We don't always welcome "progress." There's a narcotic dimension to doing things the way you've always done them. Few lawyers want to reinvent themselves (let alone continuously).

The same goes for organizations. They develop methodological inertia, or momentum; they slide about in well-worn ruts.

It's natural and good for people and groups to resist change, but certain forms are quite pernicious. You may have heard about "learned helplessness," exemplified by young elephants tied to a stake that adults would find easy to pull up. (Guess what they don't do when they grow up?) I've seen similar behavior in former engineers-turned-lawyers who don't deign to touch a keyboard or who insist upon printouts of e-mail. Or a classmate with a million-dollar-plus annual draw who could barely grab a quick lunch because a client had him on a "short leash."

Pain is more of a driver than opportunity. If you're lucky enough to already be making $400,000 per year, you're not likely to want to rock the boat. "If it's not broke . . ." Successful people are especially prone to overlooking their inefficiencies.

All knowledge tool initiatives involve some disruption, some derailing. They accordingly bump up against strong instincts and vested interests.

Okay, you can put your watch back. But remember how awkward it felt on the "wrong" arm.

Financial Practices and Organizational Structure

I used to suspect that hourly billing was the biggest obstacle to legal knowledge tools. It can certainly be a formidable challenge: why spend money to acquire tools that will result in your doing work faster when you charge by the hour? But there are lots of good answers to that question (see Chapter 22). And hourly billing is only one aspect of an entire syndrome of arrangements and attitudes that get in the way of practice modernization. Many of these are embedded in the typical financial practices and organizational structures of law firms.

It's a commonplace of organizational theory that you get the behavior you reward. And most lawyers are compensated and promoted based on how many hours they clock. They don't generally get paid for creating or sharing knowledge. (Before going on, let me acknowledge that time tracking has its clear uses and advantages. Detailed time records provide metrics that are useful in any billing regime and are especially appropriate in the absence of clear value standards.)

No one likes to feel stupid or lose power, indispensability, or strategic advantage. It can be rational to hoard knowledge and persist in inefficient methods if you lack confidence that you will be fairly rewarded for changing. There's low incentive to build skills in others.

Law firms have little tradition of knowledge capitalization. There's great reluctance to invest in things clients don't "see"—unlike carpets, fancy furniture, and offices illuminated late into the evening.

The inability of firms (under ethical rules) to fund internal investments with outside capital likewise hampers innovation.

Finally, in most offices it's not yet anyone's job to pay attention to knowledge technology specifically. No one's in charge. This tends to produce sponsor apathy.

> The Pulitzer time capsule was buried under a building in 1884. In 1954, the building was demolished and people spent sixteen months sifting through the rubble before finding it. Among its contents was the only copy of the building plan that showed the capsule's location.

Power Structure

Beneath the surface of financial practices and organizational charts lies a deeper complex of processes and values. Structural characteristics of a firm, like partner/associate ratios, likely accommodate old ways of doing things. There are generational conflicts: partners near retirement don't want to spend money on investments that won't pay until after they're gone. Outdated rules for dividing up the pie can lead to a "tragedy of the commons" in which everyone wants to take out, but no one wants to put in. Diminished loyalty to firm and greater mobility among professionals threatens to make this even worse.

Organizations tend to evolve structures, elicit behaviors, and groom leaders who perpetuate reigning organizational values. People are invested in the value structure implicit in current work arrangements and processes. There are intricate payoff systems—social hydraulics—that sustain the status quo. When disrupted, organizations tend to return to equilibrium, like the human body does under the mechanism of homeostasis.

More than other technologies, knowledge systems intrude upon very fundamental aspects of how work is organized and how rewards are divided up. You can't get far without recognizing and dealing with the preexisting internal knowledge economy. We need to evolve new mechanisms for allocational fairness in a world of shared knowledge tools.

Lawyers are reluctant to be replicated—even in part—in a system that might reduce their monopoly value. They hoard knowledge because it gives them power. They think, "If I allow too many of my precious intellectual fluids to be sucked out and be put out into a system, I'm relinquishing some of that power." It requires a leap of faith in most organizations to buy into contributions to the central good. That runs counter to the predominant ethos we see in law offices.

The Legal Personality

Part of the legal profession's resistance to using machines for our knowledge work is that we're not disposed or trained to think that way. Lawyers can be arrogant, provincial, change averse, and technophobic.

Experts differ over what personality types are most commonly found in law.

The number one personality trait of lawyers, according to a study done by Larry Richard of Altman Weil, is *skepticism.*[1] Lawyers are trained arguers and nit-pickers. They can be strong willed, stubborn, know-it-alls. Not invented here = not good enough.

Lawyers are often rugged individualists. They are jealous of professional freedom, protective of turf, territorial. They hate being managed and

---

[1] See e.g., *Herding Cats: The Lawyer Personality Revealed*, Larry Richard, Altman Weil Report to Legal Management, August 2002.

resist being held accountable. Many are autonomy cravers and control freaks. They also have a high incidence of depression, defeatism, substance abuse, divorce, and suicide.

Many of us chose the law because it is a learned profession. Most of us did well in school and enjoyed our educations. We became "professionals" because we didn't want to be "businesspeople" and deal with the crass details of commerce. If we had wanted to become engineers, we wouldn't have slept through math.

So how might these self-selected skeptics, non-techies, non-businesspeople instinctively think about knowledge tools?

- Some will feel about their knowledge being "captured" the way aborigines fear their souls being stolen by being photographed. They hear "repository" and think "suppository."

- Some will resist getting drawn into knowledge system projects because they don't want to *appear* to have free time. ("You must not have real work to do.")

- Some will resent having what they do automated (faster, better, cheaper) because of what that says about the work they *have* been doing up until then. It's threatening to ego, status, and compensation if a machine might be able to do some of that work.

- Some lawyers don't *want* to be "liberated" from routine or repetitive "drudgery" and have to do hard thinking all day.

- And, let's admit it, many lawyers find this stuff boring. Building and maintaining software systems is *not* intrinsically interesting for most.

Culture

An organization's culture is not cleanly separable from the personality types of its inhabitants; both reflect each other. But cultural resistance to knowledge technology seems to have a life of its own.

Anthropologist Jennifer James[2] makes a compelling case for viewing law firms as frat houses or lodges. Not exactly institutions that foster routinely high standards of collective behavior.

---

[2] *Thinking in the Future Tense* (1996), p. 137.

Many firms acknowledge that they are little more than solo practitioners sharing overhead. Their traditions sometimes seem like recitations of heroic personalities from the past, reminding me of the plaintive (but presumably apocryphal) oral poems of New Guinea, which consisted of nothing but the names of the tribal poets who contributed to them.

A knowledge-sharing culture is the sum of countless little actions by individuals. If you have few of those actions, you aren't going to have much of that culture.

Fear

For some, knowledge tools are downright scary. Putting aside general technophobia, we find the following:

- Fear of the unknown, of uncharted waters.
- Fear of setting things in motion that might lead to broader change (Pandora's box, slippery slope).
- Fear of failure (maybe based on the recent memory of unsuccessful efforts).
- Fear of "what else I'll have to do if I delegate the easy stuff."

Involvement in *building* knowledge tools can raise special kinds of concern:

- Fear of accountability or liability—you might fear being too candid about how something was previously handled and having it come back to haunt you.
- Fear of embarrassment or exposure—lawyers often don't want other people critically examining their work.

Difficulty

Let's not underplay the complexity and subtlety of knowledge that many legal professionals wield. Trying to surface and codify even elementary forms of tacit knowledge can be a daunting challenge. Being explicit is hard work.

There are two kinds of tacit knowledge: that which *can't* be articulated and that which can but hasn't yet been. Some people are alarmed to discover they can't really articulate what they've been doing. You might be a truly great expert but are incapable of formalizing even parts of your knowledge.

We don't just *know* things tacitly; we *think* things through at an unconscious level. Lawyering involves a lot of tacit deliberation and unconscious strategizing that is not easily surfaced. Lawyers are (usually) good at lawyering. They're not usually good at systematizing or automating their knowledge.

Difficulty also arises from the multidisciplinary nature of this work, both in terms of individuals needing to be knowledgeable in several domains and in terms of projects requiring coordinated effort across teams consisting of representatives from various disciplines. The disciplinary melting pot can include technology, management, lawyering, education, and librarianship.

Besides the cognitive difficulty of knowledge tool projects, there are social and emotional difficulties. It can be painful to harmonize practices across a work group, especially if it derived from groups at several predecessor firms or it has more than a couple of strong personalities in it. (Partner A insists on underlining defined terms while Partner B capitalizes them.)

And it's always hard to change the tires while the car is moving. Law offices don't have the luxury of shutting down for a couple weeks to retool the production line.

Ignorance and Misconception

The biggest barrier to knowledge technology adoption in law offices is likely ignorance. Most legal professionals have just not yet learned much about it and its benefits. Blame those of us who ought to be doing a better educational job. And there are also troublesome misconceptions—you might say myths—afoot. Some of these reflect the professional chauvinism touched on earlier. But mostly they represent unfortunate overgeneralizations.

 ♦ "What *I* do can't be systematized." *My* work is idiosyncratic, custom. Every client engagement is unique. Software tools may be appropriate for those folks down the hall who do a lot of routine work, but they're not suitable for the high-rate, high-value work *I* do.

The reality is that some kinds of knowledge tools make sense for virtually every practice. No one argues that the entire job most lawyers do can be automated. But inevitably large parts of the work turn out to be improvable through systems.

 ♦ "We tried it and it didn't work."

You can say that about just anything. Just what was the "it" that didn't work? Can you fairly draw absolute conclusions from one episode of failure?

Losing our Inhibitions

Motives, motivation, emotion, motion, motor, dynamo—all of these words share a root sense of movement. If we're convinced a knowledge tool destination is worthy, how do we get moving in that direction?

When you're dealing with stuff that might be perceived as important but not urgent, someone has to persuade people that personal involvement is essential. Doing so requires finding both rational and emotional motivators. Put more crassly, it requires recognizing that most people have their radio dials tuned to WIIFM ("What's in it for me?").

The following management mantras may be platitudes, but they are worth keeping in mind as strategies to maximize motivation and minimize inhibition:

- ♦ Secure high-level commitment and leadership.
- ♦ Adopt an explicit internal marketing attitude.
- ♦ Cultivate early adopters.
- ♦ Showcase successes elsewhere.
- ♦ Reward people with time credits, bonuses, even royalties.
- ♦ Use quality software and experienced developers.
- ♦ Make it fun.

So what's in it for *you*? Regardless of your practice, you can likely get better results with less effort through the appropriate use of knowledge tools. They can help you have happier clients, more money, and more job satisfaction.

If you and your colleagues aren't already enjoying many (or any) of these benefits, consider the possibility that *you* are the one holding you back. Look back over the inhibitions reviewed above. Think about which may apply to you and whether you want them to govern your future.

Interlude

Oh Say,
Can You C?

Preparing for a New Era of Legal Commerce

If you expect to be practicing law for at least a while longer, here are some ideas and suggested readings in the spirit of continuing education. I'd like to draw your attention to several C words that will likely be central to many of our careers. Remember the adage that C students are often the most successful.

Change

One need not look far for reminders of the dramatic changes facing lawyers and the profession. Multidisciplinary and multijurisdictional practices. Virtual law firms. Application service providers. Intelligent do-it-yourself legal software. We're being buffeted simultaneously by record-size waves of technological and economic transformation. The competitive context is mutating. You might say we're in the midst of a serious C change.

Recent years have seen a Cambrian explosion of new organizational life forms determined to play a role in the delivery of legal services. (For those of you who haven't read Stephen Jay Gould's *Wonderful Life*, which recounts the original Cambrian explosion in biology, I highly recommend it.) Hundreds of Web-based start-ups (upstarts?) sought to execute novel business models aimed at what lawyers and law firms have traditionally done. Online dispute-resolution services like CyberSettle, Square-Trade, and WebMediate. Reverse auctions like SharkTank and eLawForum. Self-help sites like MyLawyer and Nolo.com. Referral companies like i>path. Flat-fee service providers like AmeriCounsel and MyCounsel. Exchanges like LawCommerce. Litigation funding companies like the LawFinance Group and ExpertFunding. (Other than an inordinate fondness for intermediate capital letters, these companies exhibit a diversity as broad as many animal phyla. And it's not just little newcomers—goliaths like West and Lexis are busy growing, or buying, new organs.)

While many of these species went extinct in the wake of the capital-crunch meteor that hit in 2000, some survived and others will emerge. We heard a lot of millennial talk about the "new economy," about how the world of business was changing unrecognizably. Much of that imagined change sputtered. But despite the smugness of today's "I told you so" new-economy naysayers, fundamental opportunities for transformative innovation in how law is done remain. Just when you think the revolution has fizzled, its most significant chapters may be unfolding. Beware of post-bubble-burst complacency.

Lawyers need to be open to radically different ways of doing their jobs and embrace change as an affirmative good. (If you're short on ideas, read Gary Hamel's *Leading the Revolution* for a few hundred.) Rattle your cage a bit.

Let me address three contexts in which lawyers have to do better if they hope to survive and prosper, rather than wistfully fan the embers of good days gone by.

Clients

Clients' number one complaint about lawyers is that they don't return phone calls promptly and otherwise keep clients informed. This common courtesy in client relations is rarely taught in law school or emphasized in practice. But communicative effectiveness—both in telling *and* listening—is an obvious touchstone of professional success. It is the foundation for genuine trust. Unless you're already *sure* you're an excellent communicator, I encourage you to go way overboard in that department.

While client expectations about being kept *informed* probably haven't changed much over the years, there does seem to be a definite trend toward more client interest in being *involved* in the legal work being done on their behalf. The "unbundled" model of services, where discrete tasks like drafting, advice, court appearances, and negotiation are allocated as desired between the lawyer and client, versus the traditional, lawyer-does-all, full-service model, has a definite appeal and promising future. Many individual and business clients treasure the sense of empowerment and transparency that comes from their lawyers treating the legal work as a project undertaken in common. One manifestation of this tendency is the idea of "lawyer-client collaboratories" that I and others espoused in the early 1990s: shared workspaces online, now showing up as law firm extranets and "dealrooms."

A more general extension of the loosening of the traditional legal services bundle is the participation of third parties. Many of the dot-coms noted above positioned themselves as new kinds of intermediaries, performing collateral aspects of the legal service delivery process like engagement scoping, billing and collections, case intake, client education, routine document drafting, and case management. Even the capital to underwrite case expenses has become an ingredient that needn't come only from client or firm—witness the litigation-funding companies that have in effect created a secondary market in lawsuits.

The collaborative law movement likewise responds to these dynamics. There the parties agree in advance to eschew adversarial litigation as a process for dispute resolution and commit to cooperative problem solving, centered on four-way meetings at which both clients and their attorneys participate.

Pay attention to opportunities for closer client (and even "opponent") involvement in the legal work. Be alert to aspects of that work that can be done less expensively or more effectively by someone else. Sign up to provide services through one or more of the online exchanges. Think of your job as that of a trusted advisor to the whole process and team through which your client's legal needs are cost-effectively met.

Colleagues

Communication and collaboration with colleagues can obviously also be improved in most law offices. Knowledge-management initiatives, when in vogue, frequently founder on the unpreparedness of lawyers for sharing their work. Our personality types and institutional legacies tend to promote self-reliance and competitiveness. Our billing and compensation practices often reward wheel reinvention and knowledge hoarding. Not a recipe for thriving in a world of nimble new competitors.

Collegiality, of course, does not stop at the walls of your organization. Lawyers have a proud tradition of cooperative work through national, state, and local bar associations. Nowadays, e-mail discussion groups,

Web-based forums, and social networks provid
fruitful exchange not only around substantive
nology and other practice-management topics.
some of this, start. Get active in a practice-mar
association.

Character

After many years of tilting at these windmills, I
ever that it all comes down to personal values,
mind-sets. No amount of brilliant business pla
nology will produce enduring improvements in
enough *people* in that system embrace the need
tional change. And that's largely a matter of cu
maturity, and emotional intelligence.

The more lawyers find ways to live satisfying ar
ter off will be the rest of humanity. Take time to
transformation, to "sharpen the saw." As Maha
become the change you want to see in the worl
sic, *The Seven Habits of Highly Effective People*, de

In Closing

I would close this interlude with a call to open
We need to open our minds, our relationships,
kinds of connections. Parties prepared to be op
needs and interests can often obtain superior s
rative lawyers than traditional litigators. Lawye
what they know (and don't) stand a better cha
management systems skyrocket their organizat
software designers who observe open-source pr
their work will likewise reap the benefits of coll
unbundling of law practice into discrete tasks t
flexibly among lawyers, clients, and third parti
tization of software into interoperable, reusable
thrive on a certain degree of openness and crea

The Internet has shown us what wonderful, un
when an open infrastructure is put in place. Ch

band is ushering in a second, more dramatic round of connectivity-catalyzed developments. We are privileged to be present at a point in history when similar dynamics may be afoot in the workings of the law. Today's technology and business innovations are powerful solvents, dissolving historical bonds and boundaries, breaking old and enabling new connections of all sorts. It falls to our vision and courage to make the most of this fluidity.

Change. Client focus. Communication. Collaboration. Collegiality. Community. Common ground. Connectivity. Components. Culture. Character.

Focus your mind on these critical concepts. And don't get too distracted by e-this and e-that, B2B, P2P, etc. You'll feel much better.

C? I told you.

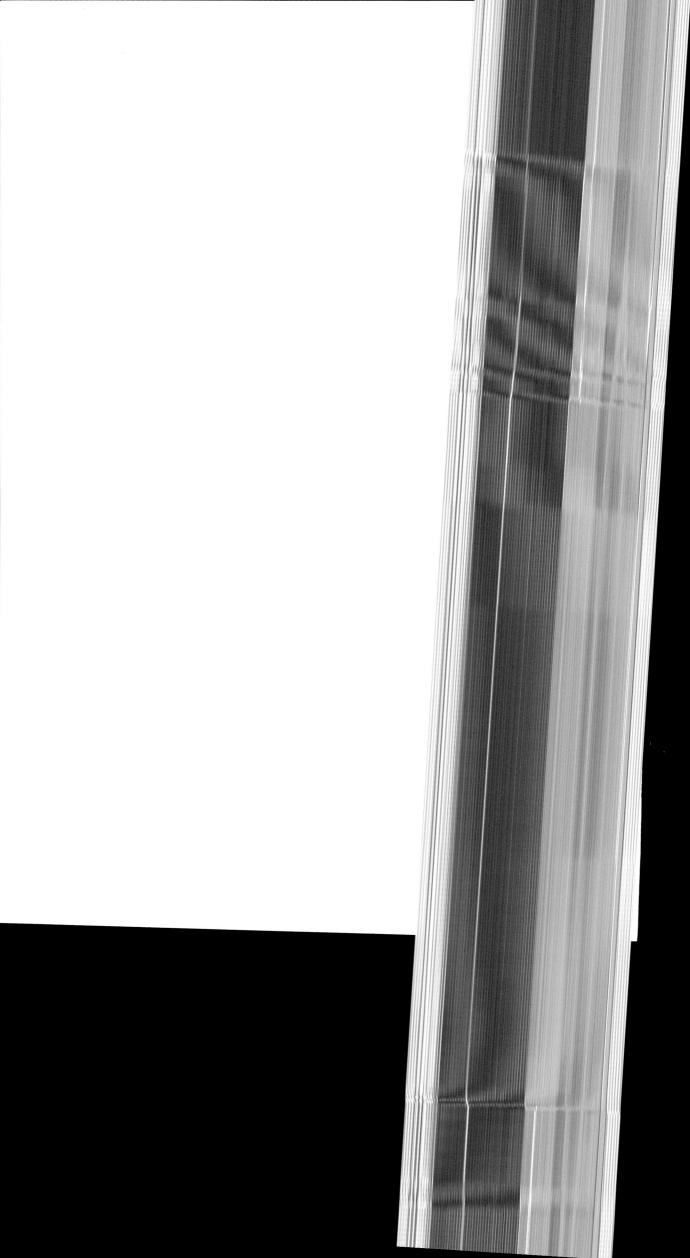

PART FOUR

How

YOU NOW KNOW *WHAT* "knowledge tools" are and *why* they can be so useful. So it's time to get into *how* they can be acquired and deployed.

In this section, we'll cover the following:

- ◆ How to find and choose tools
- ◆ When to build and when to buy
- ◆ How to build when you can't buy
- ◆ How to manage knowledge tool projects
- ◆ How to realize the financial benefits of time-saving tools in a world of hourly billing

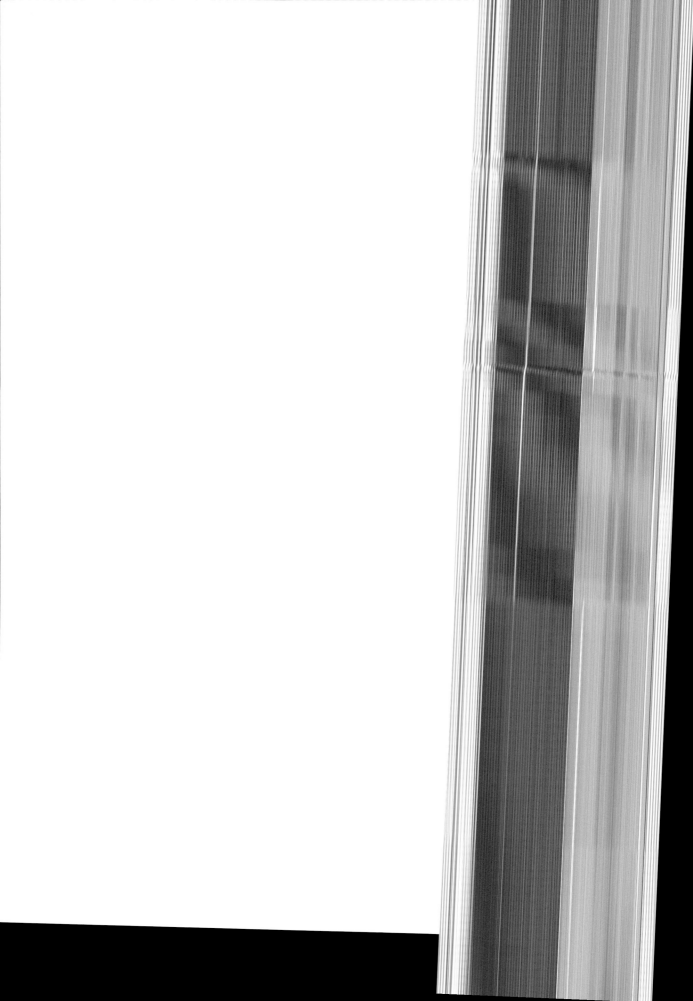

CHAPTER TWENTY

Finding and Choosing Tools

Finding Knowledge Tools

Legal knowledge tools generally don't come labeled as such, and there is no convenient paper catalog or online site that identifies them in one place. I figure that there are several thousand discrete software applications now commercially available that would fit the description and several hundred vendors and consultants offering products and services in the knowledge tools area.

There are several dozen Web sites already providing some aspects of the above information, but I know of no organized and comprehensive resource to which people can turn to find out what tools there are, what's good, what's bad, and why. The companion Web site to this book includes a list of sites and other resources (**www.SmarterLegalWork.com**).

It's always a good idea to consult fellow practitioners and bar association law practice management advisers. Pick up a couple of legal technology publications at trade conferences or practice area events. Googling key phrases like "Florida real estate form automation" will at least get you a lot of raw material.

Choosing Practice System Authoring Software

Computer-based practice systems are tools for legal workers, and authoring environments are tools for the toolmaker. Whether the toolmaker is an attorney working nights on a do-it-yourself system, a designated "com-

puter responsible person," or a consulting "knowledge engi
desirable that his or her toolbox be adequately outfitted.

Don't try to cut corners on software—it is *not* the major ex
development. People are. Software savings that reduce hum
ness are false economies of the worst sort.

Features to consider in comparing practice system authorir
alternatives include the following:

- *Integration with word processing.* Can you import and
  ted documents? With what word processing progran
  compatible? Can documents be edited and printed f
  system? Can you emulate your favorite word proces:
  tem's own editor? Can you prepare more than one d
  time?

- *Data management.* Can you save client data between
  you examine information about more than one clie
  time? Can you import from and export to external
  agement programs?

- *Ease of use.* How long does it take for a user to learn
  applications built with the system? Is the interface
  itself and with conventions used in popular softwai
  you navigate around the screens easily? Leave quest
  swered? Revise prior responses? Annotate your ansv
  remap keys to your own liking? Is there online hel[

- *Ease of authoring.* How complex is the command la
  there any automated application-generation facilit
  to compile your systems, or can they be viewed in ;
  as you build? Does the system include an interactiv
  macro facility? How easy is it to revise and update
  tions?

- *Power.* What numeric, logical, text comparison, an
  operations can the system handle? Does it support
  ing on user responses? To what extent can the autl
  content of the screens and other aspects of the use
  reference material and other resources can be mad
  user? Can such resources be global? Dynamic? Int
  textual? Can users copy text from them to paste el
  you link with and pass control to external progran
  standard programming interface to internal algori
  structures? Is there any automated explanation of

or advice? What automated text-formatting features are supported?—paragraph numbering? cross-references? list punctuation? columns? tables of contents? indexes?

♦ *Documentation, training, and support.* Is the written documentation comprehensive and comprehensible? Is training available for authors? Is there an online tutorial for users? What telephone support is there? Are there users groups and newsletters?

♦ *Continuity.* Are the product and company stable? Can you purchase the source code or arrange to have it escrowed with a third party? How many other people are using the software? Is there a significant ecosystem of users, consultants, and vendors?

♦ *Cost.* What does a license cost? Do you need a run-time license to run finished applications? Are site licenses available? What is the charge for maintenance and support? Is there a toll-free number?

This is a daunting list, to be sure. Examining several of the available packages with these kinds of questions in mind, however, can be a very instructive exercise. Most vendors are more than willing to send descriptive literature and demonstration copies of their software. Software can also often be viewed at legal technology trade shows, bar association functions, and related activities. Most important, those just starting to embark on practice-system development should locate other lawyers and offices that have already begun.

Document-Assembly Engines

There has been a dizzying variety of technologies, vendors, and approaches in the legal document–assembly universe since the late 1970s. In a recent exercise I was able to list *sixty-five* discrete engines aimed at lawyers that have been commercially available at some point. (Most are long gone.)

The last comprehensive public roundup I saw was the one Alan Soudakoff and I did for *Law Office Computing* ("Shopper's Guide to Legal Document Assembly," October/November 1997). We did a *Consumer Reports*–style analysis of ten leading products back then, covering several dozen of the most important comparative features. In more recent private analyses, we've identified hundreds of differentiating characteristics.

Here is a very brief and subjective sketch of today's leading candidates. (Disclaimer: my company is certified to consult in the first three.)

HotDocs from HotDocs Corporation (**www.hotdocs.com**)
biggest market presence and most developed ecosystem. So
the neighborhood of a half million copies have been distrib
excellent online knowledgebase, e-mail discussion list, and
community. HotDocs offers the best tool for automating gr
and has a full-featured Web implementation. The company
release significant new versions each year.

GhostFill (**www.ghostfill.com**) is a vigorous player from K
South Africa. It was integrated into the Amicus Attorney ca
ment software, branded as Amicus Assembly. It also underl
and improved construction contract software from the Am
of Architects and Drafting Wills and Trusts from West Pub
Fill has a programmer-friendly, object,-oriented open arch
ing it very easy to add functionality. It offers great flexibili
integration and can be easily hooked up to databases out o
(Note: Korbitec announced in late 2006 that it would no l
sell GhostFill in the generic document-assembly market bu
on its own content-based legal applications.)

DealBuilder from Business Integrity (**www.business-in**
purely Web-based on the user end and offers an AI-based
ronment that reduces the need for traditional template p
Precedents that are marked up in ways intelligible to subs
can often be converted automatically into interactive "m
Integrity established a beach head in the London Magic (
has made major inroads into top law departments there a
United States, building on the self-service themes covere
this book.

Rapidocs (**www.rapidocs.com**) also originated in the U
It includes innovative features that optimize it for e-comn
tions. It's also active in the non-lawyer space—see **www.d**

Exari (formerly SpeedPrecedent), from Exari Systems (**w**
is a Web-based solution with a strong commitment to op
standards, especially XML.

QShift from Ixio Corporation (**www.ixio.com**) is an Inte
tion-based application with the slogan "Smart document
demand." I think of it as a clause manager on steroids. It
underlying technologies that can take it in many differen

D3 (Dynamic Document Drafting) from Microsystems (**www.microsystems.com/d3**) is one of the latest entrants. As described in Chapter 10, it has broken new ground in terms of tight integration with Microsoft Word (2003 or newer). While possibly weak on some of the more advanced aspects of high-end document automation, such as multi-level repeats, D3 includes styles management, group security, and collaborative authoring features that aren't seen in most other products.

Perfectus (**www.perfectus.com**), **ActiveDocs** (**www.keylogix.com**), and **Pathagoras** (**www.pathagoras.com**) also deserve attention. And even though they are no longer marketed or supported, quite a few offices still use old stars like **CAPS** and **PowerTXT** or have recently converted them to contemporary platforms.

CHAPTER TWENTY-ONE

Developing Systems

ENTIRE BOOKS HAVE BEEN and will be written on the design and construction of computer-based legal practice systems. This section provides a merely cursory look at basic points to consider.

Getting Started

Perhaps the most important thing I can tell you about substantive legal automation—once you've been convinced of its dramatic potential—is to go into it with your eyes open. Many automation initiatives can be safely undertaken with modest amounts of resources and repay quick benefits. For most offices, starting with small efforts is definitely the way to go. A simple automation project will illustrate what is involved in building legal systems, help identify those on staff who are interested and competent in system building, and provide experience in one or more authoring tools.

More elaborate software-development projects require a substantial investment of money and staff time, often run behind schedule, and have a significant failure rate. If you are not prepared to allocate adequate resources to such a project, it is much better not to begin. If the investment does seem warranted, it is essential to plan carefully and monitor progress persistently.

Choosing a Subject

Some legal subjects and tasks make ideal candidates for automation; many don't. In general, an office needs to do a significant volume of

transactions of a particular sort to make automation initiati
them worthwhile. The tasks involved should be reasonably
nonetheless well enough structured to capture in computer
there must be an availability of both experts and end users
process.

First-time-final documents like confirming letters and unio
like appellate briefs are not good candidates for substantive
Patterned contracts, agreements, pleadings, discovery docu
letters are.

In fixing the scope of your project, it is useful to observe ar
i.e., be content (jubilant!) to have your system handle 80 p
cases in the area of its applicability.

Buying and Building

One pervasive question in the document-automation wor
buy or build. Should you roll your own document assemb
an existing platform? Should you develop your own *conter*
ricated templates off the shelf? Should you manage your o
environment or rent one that someone else maintains?

I hope by now that you see little benefit in creating your o
assembly tools. There are many good ones already out the
modest cost. I'm surprised and saddened when I run into
have wasted effort reinventing basic features.

On the other end, rentable document-automation envir
recently become available. Some vendors offer ASP (app
provider) solutions, where both underlying tools and de
are served to your users from off site. These hosting moo
to grow, riding a general "software as a service" trend in
For examples, see **www.directlaw.com**, **www.accudraft.**
www.estateworks.com.

But the real action is in the content area. Templates can l
accessed on a subscription basis. Before you spend a lot o
and learning a document-assembly engine, see if someor
already automated your target documents.

If you can find a practitioner-turned-DA-maniac who ha
hensive set of forms for your practice area, you may be al

them all for a fraction of what it would cost to create even a small subset independently. We've seen that phenomenon, for instance, with Ohio divorce forms (see **www.ohiodrsoftware.com**).

Estate planning is one of the richest areas in terms of prebuilt content. WealthDocs from WealthCounsel, LLC (**www.wealthcounsel.com**) and Wealth Transfer Planning from Interactive Legal Systems (**www.inter activelegal.com**) are both based on the HotDocs platform. Drafting Wills and Trust Agreements (**west.thomson.com/dwta**), recently released by West Publishing, uses GhostFill. There are dozens of others.

There are published sets for bankruptcy, real estate, immigration, incorporation, family law, construction contracts, commercial lending, civil litigation, and many other areas, often with state-specific versions. Many of these can be customized and extended.

There's not yet a good central clearinghouse of document-assembly applications, so you'll need to do some searching. Besides the obvious Internet search engines, you can find good leads from fellow practitioners, bar association law practice management consultants, legal technology publications, and practice area events.

In-Source or Outsource?

Just like the buy-versus-build issue, one issue commonly faced by document-assembly adopters is whether to accomplish their goals with in-house personnel or outside consultants.

Unless you're a large organization with dedicated practice applications staff, you're likely to be best served by engaging an outside expert. They'll save you time, money, and aggravation.

I know several dozen people with deep experience and considerable wisdom in the legal document–assembly field. Many are former practitioners. Some went into this field straight from law school. Some are former or current paralegals or legal secretaries; some are programmers or other IT professionals. There are hundreds of specialists out there with significant skills in particular products and with modest rates.

Practicing lawyers and other nonspecialists who are so inclined can often accomplish a lot of document modeling, but there's a threshold beyond which they can't realistically go in building and maintaining complex applications. Know your limits. (Or become one of the specialists!)

Building Systems

Our experiences in recent years have led my colleagues and
nize the importance of developing and following standard
substance and procedure of system building—in other wor
tematic about our systems! Such standards include a style
gramming and user interface conventions and a carefully
cle" calendar for software development. We try to gear eac
system-building project to an evolving set of written speci
are developed in cooperation with experts and end users.

While formalities of this degree may only be necessary in
where multiple systems are being built for multiple sites,
find value in something of the sort. Written "contracts" of
between users, experts, and system builders are well wort

In approaching a practice-system project, the first require
get organized. There is little a computer system can do to
practice other than to institutionalize the disorganizatio
exemplary forms, procedural checklists, and other mater
assembled and cross-correlated. Variable and conditiona
ments should be flagged and annotated. Flowcharts and
may be helpful. The details of sub-procedures and sub-p
be worked out, after which they can be linked together i
block fashion.

"Who should build practice systems?" is a common que
authoring systems aspire to reduce the need for special
indeed specific knowledge of conventional programmin
essary. Most people with sufficient interest and determi
lawyers—can become proficient system builders. Whetl
more a question of where their interests lie and where t
best deployed.

By the way, it is an illusion to suppose that "authoring"
form of "programming." The methodological insights
thought developed over the decades in other forms of
ing are unquestionably relevant. The fact that instructi
are being given in a high-level language does not alter
of the programming activity. So it seems fair to say tha
mers" who become effective system builders are no lor
grammers.

There is also little reason why specific *legal* training is necessary for a system builder. Non-lawyers can be quite effective in structuring and automating legal knowledge gathered from others. An expert practitioner with incentive is an essential ingredient, though, whether or not he or she is also the programmer. In most situations, the best author of a practice system is a *team* of one or more specialists in both law and in programming and analysis.

Deployment, Maintenance, and Support

Even systems that are fully tested and responsive to important office needs and have been developed in close consultation with both experts and eventual users are not self-implementing. Introducing them effectively into a busy practice requires planning and tact. Users need to be trained, computers may need to be reconfigured, and office procedures need to be adapted. Inadequate attention at this stage can counteract valiant efforts earlier in the development process.

Similarly, ongoing maintenance and support of systems needs to be planned and budgeted. No system can escape the necessity of periodic revalidation, correction, improvement, and updating. Responsibility for maintenance and support must clearly be within the scope of someone's job. Mechanisms for user feedback and regular checking for legal and tactical correctness should be established. Anticipating the need and providing for the means to maintain systems are key aspects of their design.

Scoping a Document-Assembly Project

No two document-assembly projects are the same, even within the same organization. Here are ways projects differ. Where does yours fit?

	Your Project:
Users—Who are the intended users of the application? Lawyers, paralegals, secretaries, students, clients? Are they experts in the area in question, or novices? Are they a few or many? Do they work in proximity, or are they spread among floors, offices, or cities?	

	Your Project:
Documents—What documents is the system designed to produce? Short and simple, long and complex, or somewhere in between? Are they typically first-draft-final, or do they require lots of post-assembly editing? Are official, graphical forms involved? Are the documents typically produced individually or in related sets? Can they be neatly handled with fill-in-the-blanks variables and alternative/additional passages, or do they involve lots of material that doesn't lend itself to straightforward rules?	
Scope—What range of transactions is the system intended to support? How deep do you intend to go in modeling the variations from transaction to transaction? Is the system designed only to produce first drafts or to guide users through several stages of revision and negotiation? Should it offer project-management and decision-support features?	
Purposes—What are the driving goals of the application? To speed up processing? Improve quality or consistency? Achieve greater capacity? Allow work to be delegated to more efficient staffing levels? Assist in training?	
Novelty—Is this your organization's first effort of this kind or one among several? Are the team members experienced in this kind of thing? There are vast differences between doing a first project of this kind and later ones. They involve different states of organizational and personal readiness.	
Staffing—Is the project being done entirely with in-house personnel, by an outside consultant, or some blend? Is it conceived as a project by lawyers in a practice group, aided by others, or as an initiative of the IT department, aided by lawyers?	

CHAPTER TWENTY-TWO

Making Money from Technology That Saves Time

The Productivity Paradox

Imagine completing the paperwork for typical transactions three or four times faster. Improvements like that are common with contemporary document-assembly software.

Imagine your associates finishing due diligence projects twice as fast. Efficiency gains like that are possible with intelligent checklists.

Imagine clients handling aspects of what you do, getting (and paying for) results they need with little of your time. That's now very doable with online knowledge tools.

Could *you* make good use of such improvements? What's the catch?

Law offices can skyrocket their productivity through new technologies, but the fiscal payoffs are not obvious. In an hourly-billing world, greater efficiency can mean *lower* billables. Why invest in time-saving tools when time is what you charge for?

Many lawyers face this productivity paradox. The faster they work, the less money they make for a given assignment. There is a built-in tension between efficiency-improving technology and strict hourly billing. But there is also a built-in tension between inefficiency and business prosperity.

Here are ways creative lawyers have found to unleash the profit-enhancing power of specialized practice tools. The first set is for those who con-

tinue to bill hourly. The second set is for those who are will
bill in different ways. A third section covers techniques tha
kinds of people.

How to Make Money by Saving Time even
by the Hour

Maybe you're not ready to walk away from the billable hou
that stop you from working smarter and improving your b

1. Reduce the Hours You Don't Bill for Anyway.
First, think about all the money you lose because you writ

Good systems can help eliminate some of the time you fee
write off because a timekeeper recorded more hours for a t
justified or because the overall bill seemed too high. Or be
complained.

"Hidden caps" on bills are common. Explicit caps are incr
causing pain when accidentally over-run—and nail biting
cally under-set.

2. Improve Work Conditions for People Whose Ti
Don't Bill.
Don't forget that efficiencies for staff whose time is neve
secretaries, can straightforwardly reduce operating costs.
automation can radically improve word processing effici
mizing errors and frustration. Being able to make do wit
staff—who are happier and stay longer—could do wond
head.

3. Get More Business.
Practice automation can strengthen client service, qualit
competitive advantage and reduce costs. Offering high-q
with faster turnaround is a proven way to attract more bu
ogy investments can help draw business. You can pitch t
ments to clients, put them in proposals and bids, and hi
your Web site.

Perhaps you have unused capacity you'd be happy to put
of a promising new client, even if the effective hourly rat
you ordinarily demand.

4. Keep Business You Might Otherwise Lose.

Sometimes you have a book of business that is not especially profitable but for strategic reasons would be costly to lose. Sometimes your anchor clients are actively shopping for better prices and services elsewhere. You can't afford not to innovate.

Corporate counsel in particular are increasingly demanding controls on outside legal costs. Loyalty will not stop them from moving work elsewhere if your charges are too high. One partner at a large New York firm once told me that using document assembly is "the only way to stay competitive."

5. Add a Transaction Fee to Recover Technology Costs.

Document-automation pioneer Eric Little recommended that firms add on a per-transaction cost that has the effect of roughly splitting the billable time savings between firm and client. Systems can be viewed as hypothetical banks of time that can be drawn down across many transactions. You make deposits of time as you create and maintain them, and you make withdrawals—with interest—as you use them. Reductions in hours billed are more than made up for in transaction fees.

6. Raise Your Rates for Work that Leverages Automated Expertise.

Do you find that you're being forced to bill at too low a rate? That operating costs are escalating, profits are being squeezed, and yet you don't dare raise rates?

Systems that demonstrably enhance your professional effectiveness can help justify higher rates. Again, quality work done quickly is worth more than work of lesser quality or speed.

Blair Janis, a legal technologist in Utah, describes the result as follows: "Individual clients pay less than they would have without the automation [fewer hours for that client], but the lawyer continues to bill the same number of hours overall at a higher rate than before [getting more work done for more clients in the same amount of time it took without the automation]."

How to Make Even More Money Through Value Billing

You've probably noticed that some of the most valuable things you do for clients are not fairly measured by the amount of time they take. And that an hourly approach penalizes you for becoming more efficient on com-

modity tasks. Value-based billing opens new windows of p[
nity on both fronts.

1. Use the New Technologies in Contexts Where E
Practices Already Directly Reward Greater Prod

There are, of course, many sectors of the legal profession wl
billing is *not* dominant. Some practice areas—like continge
tion, consumer bankruptcy, immigration, no-fault divorce:
ning, and municipal finance—already have a tradition of fi
exceed fees. In most of these contexts, the basic economic
simple: given the volume of work you do (or could do), an(
savings you could realize by deploying productivity-enhan
there an adequate return on investment for the costs of th(

Fortunately, many offices recognize quick payoffs from pr
ization. Carolyn Manteuffel, with a St. Paul, Minnesota–b
injury firm that makes extensive use of document assemb
"Because we operate on a contingency fee basis, efficienc
the game. The more the staff can crank out, the more file
handle at one time, the more money we make."

2. Charge for the Time It *Used* to Take You Befor

Many lawyers engage in de facto value billing: they charg
task ordinarily would have taken, or should have taken, e
pened to have actually spent more time (or less time, bec
has recently been done for another client). Absent clear (
any significant "hypothetical" time accounting like this
concerns. But with client consent, arrangements like the
everyone's interests.

Nancy Grekin, a Honolulu practitioner, notes:

> Pigs get fed and hogs get slaughtered. If a lawyer charges t
> client will complain, and it doesn't take bar association et
> dards for the lawyer to figure that out. I see the billing for
> documentation as the amortization of the lawyer's time a
> in creating that document and turning out something th
> and is what the client wants and needs.

3. Set flat Rates for Service Packages that Are
to Automation.

If the competition keeps busy doing a certain kind of w
price of $X without any significant use of knowledge-l(

ogy, power-tool-equipped providers should be able to do that work at a significant discount from $X and still make a profit. One straightforward way is to specify fixed prices for well-defined service components or packages. If automating lets you do a job in one-half or one-third the time it ordinarily would take, charge a flat fee that is perhaps 10–15 percent lower than the average fee pre-automation and you can make a lot of money.

"What if everybody did this?" you ask. "Wouldn't that eventually force prices down?" Welcome to the free-market economy. But given the glacial pace so far of billing innovation in the legal profession, you needn't worry too much. In the meantime, there are great opportunities for early adopters.

Nancy Grekin notes that document assembly

> can produce huge premium billing. Most of what I do with my auto-mated documents are matters that I charge a flat fee for, so the hourly rate is not important. The charge ends up being something far larger than my usual hourly rate, however, because of the efficiency of produc-ing the document (some might argue obscenely higher) but it doesn't result in a charge that the client thinks is unfair or too high. And when I do use automated documents in connection with a larger matter, I may end up charging more for the transaction than the hourly amount results in if I think the result was worth it.

How to Make Money Either Way

1. Think Long Term.
Be sure to consider the contributions to firm quality and productivity that go beyond the immediate bottom line, such as training new attor-neys, capturing knowledge of staff who leave, reducing errors, and mak-ing practice less dreary. Quality-of-life improvements like these will more than pay for themselves over the long run.

2. Ask Clients to Underwrite Some Costs of Your Technology.
Think of billing as the process through which clients are asked to con-tribute appropriately to the cost of services they receive. Given the oppor-tunity, long-term clients may well be happy to help underwrite technolo-gies that allow you to deliver services they need more cost-effectively. Not only will that help you serve them better with little out-of-pocket cost, but the results can often be put to profitable use elsewhere.

One top firm arranged for a client to fund the developmen
edge base underlying a system, which was independently v
client, and then sold systems based on that work to other f
departments, and a publisher.

3. Consider Hybrid Scenarios.

None of these approaches needs be pursued in isolation, a
rally go hand in hand. For instance, Lee Knight, an indepe
oper of document-assembly applications based in San Die

> One of my clients (a group of estate planning attorneys and
> realized that to take advantage of document-assembly effic
> had to change their billing practice from an hourly rate sys
> combination of (1) fixed per-document charges (varying a
> the type of document) and (2) per-hour counseling charge
> exceeding the baseline for preparation of those document
> time to figure out the charges, but the new system is work
> client's clients seem to like the new system because it give
> definitive idea of what their costs will be.

According to Diane M. Smith, of Napa, California–based
Smith, Myers & Miroglio,

> Our law firm gets through the "penalty" for faster comple
> ments by charging a flat rate for a particular service and c
> hourly rate for any additional work or conferences, etc. F
> the estate planning, the flat rate for a "trust package" car
> to $5,000, depending on the complexity of the documer
> of trusts. Our fee letters list for the quoted flat rate, most
> documents associated with a trust plan. We also quote a
> (the rate depending on which attorney is handling the n
> additional services, such as assistance in funding the tru
> preparation of beneficiary designation forms for the clie
> or insurance plans or recording real property.

A Good Example

An attorney in the Midwest gave me the following repor

> I recently started doing loan documentation for a natio
> lender. The fees are paid by the borrower, but the lende
> the borrower to get angry about the fees. Part of the ove

the bank is that our lawyers are smart and reasonable. While there probably hovers about these deals the sense that the work is hourly, in fact every deal charges out about the same. I call in my fees to the closing secretary, and they are paid out of closing, and I have never had a borrower ask to see documentation of any kind. I send bills to nobody. Clearly the bank and the borrower have a sense that value is being delivered on a per-transaction basis and therefore do not think to inquire into the details. The details do not matter. This is no doubt because the prior law firm used was charging about $18,000 per deal, and I, thanks in part to the efficiencies of HotDocs, charge more in the $8,500 to $9,500 range. If I could generate 500 loans per year, I could service them all and make the clients very happy and, frankly, print money.

Incidentally, we manage these loans this way: I generate the documents and convert them to PDF and send to all interested parties via e-mail. Comments come back via e-mail. Once final documents are agreed to (with the quality control of HotDocs, comments and revisions decline through time), original signature pages are signed in various cities, overnighted to the closing secretary who then prints out my PDF documents and assembles the final documents. Rarely do the parties need to talk by phone, and I have never met many of the lawyers with whom I do business routinely. This sounds simple, but it was a revelation to the bank and to the borrowers. It is just so much easier than the old way. It was in part because we brought this to the bank and because of our comfort with all of this that the bank and borrowers saw us as the go-to guys. I could serve any lender in the United States with similar business and never miss a beat, no matter where they are located.

Doing Well by Doing Good

Advanced technologies can richly reward firms that figure out how to leverage them. Often an hourly-billing mind-set gets in the way of both profitability and client satisfaction. But you don't need to jettison current billing arrangements to do better.

Lawyers tend to under-invest in technologies that enhance their effectiveness. Not enough of them have figured out how to profit from practice technology, and until they do, our whole profession will fail to live up to an important aspect of its potential. Making money from working smart as well as working hard is a recipe not only for lawyer prosperity but for the effectiveness of the legal system.

Clients crave quality, attentive service, predictability, and g
the long run, lawyers who use the latest tools and techniqu
will get the work—and the results—they deserve. Let's see
down, bring revenues up. Sounds like a formula for profit—
bill by the hour or not.

Going Deeper

Robertson, Mark A., and James A. Calloway. *Winning Alter*
Billable Hour: Strategies That Work, 3rd ed., Chicago: Am
ciation, 2008.

Interlude

Smart Pads on the Wireless Web

Magic Carpet Ride

It's an old dream: You wield a magic yellow pad, its pages rippling with intellectual current. Case information and legal research display on command. You save scribbled notes for easy search and retrieval. All your files can be called up from anywhere and at any time. Checklists and questionnaires reshape themselves as you work. Phone and videoconferences just require a couple of taps.

Okay. Let's be a little more realistic. How about a lightweight, pad-shaped device that's intuitive to use, reasonably unobtrusive, wirelessly networked, and equipped with some pretty smart software?

Three developments have gotten us a lot closer to that dream:

- A new generation of tablet PCs
- Wi-Fi
- Web-enabled knowledge tools

Put them together and compelling applications become feasible. Will they change how *you* work?

Dynamic Trio

Each basic dimension of information technology has undergone several mini-revolutions in recent years:

- **Interface**—Computer use has become more intuitive as graphical interfaces, hypertext, Web browsers, and voice-recognition systems

have arrived. We're comfortable with touchscreens a
port check-in stations. Tablet PCs build on these adv
pen- (or stylus) based modes of interaction. Now we
handwriting recognition, gestural communication,
ink." (I won't attempt a full description of the tablet
have been plenty of introductory articles in trade m
the Web. If you haven't tried one yet, think of some
bines the portability of a PDA with the functionalit
model laptop, costing under $2,000. Its operating sy
cial version of Windows, and there are tablet-aware
Word, Excel, Outlook, and PowerPoint. Some law o
tech vendors are seriously evaluating these devices.

- **Connectivity**—Our ability to exchange informati
  with others has likewise steadily improved. Local a
  gave way to wide area networks and eventually the
  have the "pipes" and protocols to move data error
  some speeds. Cheap, fast wireless Internet connect
  the latest wave. Most tablet PCs include an integra
  Fi) wireless card, and Wi-Fi "hotspots" proliferate.
  geographical coverage will continue to improve. B
  tens of megabytes per second are within reach. We
  connected without all those damn connectors!

- **Intelligence**—The ability of software to do thing
  as "smart" also has been on the rise. Artificial inte
  expert systems go way back, even though practica
  have been slow in coming. In the legal world we r
  inferencing systems (like Jnana) and Web-based d
  bly tools (like DealBuilder, Exari, and HotDocs) th
  great deal of know-how and perform complex ana
  generation tasks. Knowledge-based applications e
  interactive user experiences and increasingly do
  tual labor. Online advisors step people through i
  sions and activities; intelligent templates can ass
  documents and elaborate sets.

Togetherness

Each mentioned technology independently lets us do
things. Tablet PCs are liberating even without Internet

programmed legal intelligence. You don't need pen-based interfaces or smart software to enjoy the benefits of wirelessness. You can do highly sophisticated document assembly from a fixed computer, using a conventional keyboard and mouse.

But interesting stuff starts to happen when you combine the developments. Tablets *and* wireless network access. (Why rummage around for paper files when rushing off to a meeting if their contents are somewhere online? Ever want to keyword search your handwritten notes from the *last* meeting?) Pen computing *and* document assembly. (Why fill out a paper form when you can do it in digital ink, not have to answer anything twice, and instantly route your answers to the right destination?)

Put all three together—intuitiveness and wirelessness and intelligence—and the fireworks really start. Long-mooted modes of eLawyering finally become practical.

Combinatorial Explosions

Here are just a few examples of how you might put these combined innovations to use.

- **Interviewing and counseling clients.** You can unobtrusively run an interactive questionnaire on a tablet during a client interview, maybe prepopulated with information entered by the client the day before via your firm's Web site. Or take notes in a dynamic outline. You can rapidly check and update case-management information using software like Clio or Rocket Matter.

- **Depositions.** You can likewise access a deponent-specific question outline, based, for instance, on a plaintiff's peculiar work or medical history or an expert witness's supposed expertise. If an answer surprises you, detailed follow-up questions will be right at hand. In multiparty litigation, both questionnaires and answers can be quickly shared with fellow counsel, consolidating the best thinking on key lines of investigation.

- **Due diligence work.** Associates or paralegals off site on due diligence errands can be equipped with intelligent checklists that both minimize missed issues and provide instant data uploads back to the firm, when time may be of the essence for pending transactions. Checkboxes, menus, buttons, and similar controls on such applications lend themselves well to pens.

♦ **Trials.** A small, light, easy-to-read device that resem
will likely turn out to be handy in witness examinati
ing arguments. You can check off points as you make
quick notes, and be alerted to dangerous omissions.
or instant-message notes with colleagues at counsel
the office, without those annoying clicking sounds
geek. You can generate motions, proposed offers, an
agreements on the spot.

♦ **Negotiations and closings.** With a smart tablet i
and your colleagues (or counterparties) can do colla
ing, highlighting, and annotating documents just ir
minute revisions. Need to regenerate those three hu
paper for the loan closing because a guarantor has b
or other terms have changed? No problem: fire up y
assembly program, access the latest answer file on y
the changes, assemble, and send to a convenient pr

You can imagine many other possibilities without much t
application you have or wish you had, and picture using i
a portable tablet, aided by software that seems to think ar
work. If this very book had been designed for interactivity
here to see a quick video of legal tablets in action and *here*
through an interactive analysis of how they might cost-ef
introduced into your practice, all while grabbing a bite be
O'Hare.

What's Stopping Us?

Much, of course, remains to be done. Tablets aren't as lig
itive as real yellow pads and pens. They aren't as pleasant
printed books and magazines. (But "smart paper" is eme
research labs.) And legal-tech vendors have yet to adjust
optimal performance in tablet modes.

Handwriting recognition, like voice recognition, still ma
mistakes—90 percent accuracy may be amazing, but it's
inadequate. Network bandwidth and security features ar
We need more hotspots and unquestioned data integrity

Finally, interactive checklists and intelligent templates c
to build and maintain. We'll want ready knowledge tool

new devices. An open marketplace of prefabricated applications, starter kits, and componentry is my personal dream.

Tapping and Tipping

Not all legal computing is best done on tablets. Other visions of mobile and distributed computing will contend for adoption. And no technical or market advances will neutralize deep-seated resistance to transformation. Some lawyers won't change even when full-size portable devices weigh less than an ounce, regularly get 100 Mb/sec, and cost so little as to be disposable. But most have a lower threshold.

I've long believed that we've barely begun to see the impact of IT on law practice. The confluence of technologies discussed here has produced a rare opportunity for Big Change—one of those famous tipping points at which things suddenly shift seismically. Sometimes the future sneaks up on you. This particular roller coaster may be cresting. Enough legal professionals doing enough work with smart software on wireless tablets may unleash cascades of innovation. Consider tapping into it.

PART FIVE

When

OKAY, NOW THAT YOU know who's who, what knowledge tools are, why they are worth understanding and using, and how to work with them, the remaining question is, "When?"

When might these tools begin to have a more noticeable impact on the profession and the legal system?

And when should you start putting these tools to use in your own practice?

CHAPTER TWENTY-THREE

Tomorrow

IT IS INTERESTING TO consider how the growing use of knowledge tools might change law practice itself. The possible scenarios spread out in many, often inconsistent directions. Here are speculations on a few common themes.

Just as prior technologies (typewriter, telephone, copier, word processor) unsettled the earlier balance of roles and responsibilities among workers in the law office, knowledge tools will have complex repercussions in this area. As typewriters displaced scribes and word processors threatened the traditional secretary with obsolescence, these tools will supplant growing shares of the work of lawyers themselves. Ironically, the same technology that obviated certain support staff and paraprofessional roles may now reinvigorate them. Lawyers will come to delegate more functions they have traditionally regarded as distinctively theirs.

The widespread availability of legal-practice systems will raise many nice questions. When should they be used by pro se litigants? Can the distribution of practice systems to laypeople be attacked as the unauthorized practice of law? Who is liable when use (or misuse) of a system results in malpractice? Can lawyers be held responsible for *failing* to employ available technologies, when their use could have prevented errors or produced better results? The courts and law reviews are just beginning to address these kinds of questions.

New tools and methods for doing legal work will catalyze major transformations of familiar legal institutions. Here are five:

The courthouse. Most of the solemn ceremonies of the law still take place in physical buildings. That is where judges and juries judge, witnesses tes-

tify, lawyers argue, and observers watch—for the most part
about to become much more intangible.

The general public has become more familiar with trial pro
the intense media coverage and gavel-to-gavel television ai
criminal trials such as the O. J. Simpson murder prosecutio
these exotic trials offer a fair or socially productive view of
process is open to debate.) People are coming to expect sig
dramas to be viewable from their living rooms—or at least
covered—as they happen. "Open to the public" may increa
"reported online in real time." Many courts have already b
videoconferencing and data networks in aid of efficient ad
Radical publicity of judicial activity may be unleashed as a
operational reengineering.

As a natural correlate of electronic filing, courts have begu
their records available over the Internet. Even though all
that will eventually be so provided has long been open to
principle, in reality the barriers to access (distance, specia
edge, cumbersome retrieval) have been so high as to make
ble for all but the most determined. Now it seems only a n
before virtually all current filings, and perhaps much hist
will be universally available. Except where administrative
considerations are prohibitive, there seems every likeliho
records and proceedings blending seamlessly into the dig
domain.

The law library. Although laws and legal materials have th
available to all in modern, open societies, the average nor
had an easy time getting his or her hands on relevant info
nal collections in local public libraries are often incomple
date. Unless you work for a law firm or corporation, comp
to legal sources has required a trip to a large university or
library.

Today various commercial, academic, governmental, and
tions are rushing to make primary legal material (statutes
cases) available at low or no cost on the Web. Most signifi
will soon be instantly available freely or inexpensively to
needs them. In a sense, every home and office will have a
library.

Publishers and other actors are starting to post interactive
models of that material. Simple legal expert systems use f

well-structured legal rules to drive question-and-answer tools, available online, that consumers and businesses can consult for basic guidance on their rights and duties. Publishers will market sophisticated systems like this, and there will be an escalation of even more sophisticated development inside some law offices. Some of these systems will find their way to a broader market because it often makes economic sense for holders of this valuable intellectual capital to distribute it widely.

Basic improvements in the performance and reliability of the Internet will continue to accompany these developments, resulting in perhaps as little as ten years in the availability of interactive legal content that is nearly ubiquitous and effectively instantaneous. Lawyers and non-lawyers alike will have ready access to this vast library of legal knowledge, embellished by increasingly useful indices, maps, commentaries, and other kinds of "metacontent" that provide orientation and interpretation. (Of course, there will inevitably be many differing, and even contradictory, accounts of *the* law.)

The Web now offers all kinds of astonishing information services for free, such as sites that will draw a detailed map of any neighborhood and that provide step-by-step directions for driving from one location to another. How long will it be before someone starts to provide analogous maps and directions for getting from one legal situation to another? "Where do you want to go today?" Routine legal guidance is being given away for free, paid for by advertising.

Lawyers' privileged access to legal content is necessarily eroded by these developments. Basic forms of legal information and redress are becoming available to citizens without an intervening priesthood. As this disintermediation proceeds, some lawyers who have simply been middlemen will join cars salesmen and bank tellers in the unemployment line. (Some of them may find low-paying work as "checkers" who review the transcripts of online sessions in which consumers receive computer-generated advice and documents.)

The law office. Just ten years ago we used to joke about the prospect of lawyers "hanging out shingles" in cyberspace. (There goes the neighborhood.) It was to be expected that some lawyers and firms would promptly take advantage of new forms of publicity available on the Web. This has happened in very substantial numbers. Now more and more lawyers are adopting cyberspace not merely as a medium through which to advertise their services but as a place of business: a virtual work space, or tool shed, that is potentially open around the clock and around the world. Lawyers are finding and serving clients through the Net.

Web-based initiatives have blossomed in the legal field. La deployed intelligent extranets with which clients can inter liminary advice on an automated, 24/7 basis. And commer have emerged to deliver substantially new forms of Interne service delivery.

The law school. By some measures, formal legal education h quite a bit in the last several decades. We have seen an exp tive courses dealing with history, policy, and interdisciplir Clinical fieldwork, simulation, and other kinds of experier have been introduced. Student bodies are much more ethr ually diverse.

But in many respects, legal education today is not dramati from that of the 1870s: groups of neophytes being taught Socratic classroom dialogs to "think like a lawyer" so that learned profession.

What would a "law school for tomorrow" be like? At least term future, it seems to me that it will need to pay much attention to the systems of knowledge within which and graduates will necessarily practice. It will need to make ch focus of investigation and scholarship, perhaps even to th feel comfortable talking about a "jurisprudence of chang tion should be engaged with the realities of contemporar practices, both as subjects of attention and as ongoing so dents. Law school will be a re-entrant phenomenon: peo practice, then study some more, then practice some mor episodic doses of continuing legal education should natu true lifelong learning, where lawyer/students are perpetu one or more law schools.

Some law schools will certainly also need to become gen with multiple international campuses glued together by works. Law teaching will naturally be carried out with th the groves, of cyberspace. We will have virtual campuses and seminar participation via telepresence.

At a time when traditional legal education may seem in cence, it may be offered its most important mission ever ifying and systematizing knowledge indeed becomes the professional success and a key enabler of the continuing ing and teaching reemerge as critical processes. (Learnin most ancient form of knowledge capitalization.) Lawyers themselves will not only continuously learn in order to adapt to pervasive change; they will not get far without being able to instruct their advanced information systems. And the learning organizations we've heard so much about in recent years will be commonplace.

Software (or information system) design will come to be a significant part of legal education and practice. Part of what lawyers will be known for is design information tools, processes, institutions, and environments. What is now the province of "techies," consultants, and other specialists may become the common experience of every lawyer. Programming (perhaps known by a less off-putting name) will become as common a means of communication among people and their intermediating machines, as writing has been throughout history. There may be some place for lawyers who refuse or fail to become proficient in this new communication skill, but there won't be much of a place.

The legal marketplace. We can't assume that information proficiency will spread evenly throughout the legal profession in quick order. Our practices do not have the same velocity of change as the surface technologies. We should in fact anticipate a growing lag between technological possibility and practical realization and a growing discrepancy among lawyers in the degree to which they take advantage of new forms of knowledge systematization.

Consumers of legal services are, of course, also consumers and providers of other goods and services. Even if law-practice technology lags behind other sectors, clients are noticing improvements elsewhere and expect the law to keep up. More and more clients are technology literate, familiar and comfortable with abstract information-management concepts and processes. They expect lawyers to be able to marshal relevant knowledge quickly and find mere information frictionlessly.

There is more intense competition both within and without the legal profession. The globalization of businesses, including professional services like law, is becoming an accomplished fact. The market for legal information products and services will be a substantially more efficient one. The boundaries between lawyers, accountants, consultants, and other service providers will continue to blur. It seems likely that some lawyers will find themselves in a perpetual, worldwide auction for legal services.

In short, if you expect change to plateau or slow down, expect to be disappointed.

Going Deeper

Kurzweil, Raymond, *The Singularity Is Near*, New York: Peng

Susskind, Richard, *The End of Lawyers*, New York: Oxford U
  2008.

CHAPTER TWENTY-FOUR

Today

WHEN SHOULD YOU START?

Now.

Or at least tomorrow.

Seriously.

I realize I've given you more questions than answers. But I hope you have found this book informative and inspirational. Whether or not that's true, I'd love to hear your reactions. Write me at marc@capstonepractice.com.

Here are specific things you can do:

- ♦ Take time *now* to look back through this book. What ideas struck you as intriguing, or at least plausible? What suggestions resonated with you?
- ♦ Complete the worksheets if you haven't already. Which directions seem most promising?
- ♦ Pick at least one idea to follow up on. Find someone who has already been there and done that. Call a vendor and get a trial copy of their software or arrange a demo. Attend a legal technology conference.
- ♦ Make a commitment to yourself to actually get *some* new knowledge tool in place in your own practice. Pick a specific date and write it here:

    → _____

- Keep a notebook. How often do you find yourself sa[...] stupid" or "There's got to be a better way"? Write it [...] you despair about ever changing things. Be vigilant [...] getting work of even or better quality done with onl[...] the wear and tear on *you*. Run through the implicit [...] a situation in which a little present pain (e.g., work [...] will yield lots of future gain?

- Pass this book to a colleague or buy another copy an[...] Spread the word. Enlist your fellow workers in disco[...] using better tools.

Thanks for listening.

Appendix

Book Reviews

The following reviews by the author—slightly edited—summarize five books that have tackled important aspects of knowledge technology in the legal sector.

Advanced Information Systems for Lawyers

By Vijay Mital and L. Johnson
Chapman & Hall (London), 1992
306 pages

[This review originally appeared in the ABA's *Document Assembly and Practice Systems Report*, Vol. 4, No. 4 (Summer 1992)]

Lawyer-oriented applications of technologies—like document assembly, hypertext, expert systems, conceptual retrieval, and neural networks—have largely been followed by disjointed user communities, with their own newsletters, conferences, and concerns. Publications in these fields have tended to be either shallow treatments in the trade press and bar journals or theory-laden dissertations and research conference proceedings.

While there is an abundance of general surveys of law office automation, cutting-edge subjects are mostly treated in isolation from each other and any concrete deployment. It is thus refreshing and encouraging to see an entire book published that not only consolidates a wide range of distinctively advanced "front office" legal technologies but that does so in a practical way, grounded in real-world concerns and mainstream experiences.

Vijay Mital is a leading legal technologist in Great Britain and director of the Centre for Computers in Law and Finance at Brunel University.

L. Johnson is the dean of the faculty of science and head of the Computer Department at Brunel. Together they have assembled a rich mixture of background discussion, case studies, and thoughtful analysis. Whether or not the book lives up to its claim of being accessible to readers lacking a substantial backing in information technology, it certainly provides satisfying reading for legal-tech aficionados. It is elegantly written by people who know what they are talking about and is quite up-to-date.

The focus throughout the book is on "practice support systems"—i.e., those that directly assist in the substantive practice of law. The introductory chapter discusses the nature and benefits of substantive legal technology and offers an introduction to computers and software, information systems, and specific topics like hypertext and object orientation. Part One ("Technological Foundations") covers basic concepts of artificial intelligence, including knowledge representation, knowledge acquisition, system architecture, and development methodologies. Part Two ("Applications") organizes its chapters into sections on document drafting and assembly, litigation support, and automated legal reasoning. The closing chapters discuss both the theory of neural networks and their application to legal reasoning and information-retrieval tasks. A substantial glossary and long list of references (many likely new to most American readers) are supplied.

By aspiring to meet the needs of a diversely qualified international audience of lawyers, managers, technologists, and students, Mital and Johnson took on a task destined to fail in some respects. The document-assembly chapters are exceptional so far as they go (there is special attention to hypertext-based approaches to drafting, or "intelligent brief banks"), but I would like to have seen a broader discussion of the specific tools and methodologies in use in this maturing industry. I noticed a number of significant works of recent vintage missing from the references and loose seams between specific legal applications and concerns and broader computer science discussions. Others may find disproportion in the attention given to one theme or another or occasional haphazardness in the exposition. But all readers will discover new ideas, insights, and information here. *Advanced Information Systems for Lawyers* falls short of being a definitive treatment of its subject technologies, but it is a useful and important work that deserves our attention. I highly recommend it to people who want to acquire or renew fluency with the topics that will likely dominate legal technology developments in this decade.

Law in a Digital World

By M. Ethan Katsh
New York: Oxford University Press, 1995
294 pages

[This originally appeared in the ABA's *Network2d*, Winter 1996, p. 2]

Most readers of this newsletter spend a good deal of time trying to make productive use of information technology *in* the practice of law, and many of us deal professionally with the law *of* computers and communications. These two sides of the law/computer coin are glittering these days, and the associated literatures are vast and growing. But there are yet other aspects of the interaction. One important one concerns the ways in which law—as a social institution and as a profession—is being changed *by* information technology. *Law in a Digital World* is primarily concerned with those phenomena.

Ethan Katsh—a law-trained University of Massachusetts professor who is familiar to many legal Internauts due to his presence on Lexis Counsel Connect, legal listservs, and other cyber-haunts—has devoted much of his academic attention to the impact of new media on the law. His 1989 book on the subject (*The Electronic Media and the Transformation of Law*) examined the links between law and changing media of communication. In that book he traced many attributes of modern law—such as the concept of precedent, the legal profession, and certain information law doctrines—to the aftermath of the Gutenberg revolution. The displacement of printed material by electronic media was projected to have similarly profound repercussions in law. This latest book carries those themes forward. Among other things, in the meantime (the book was completed in the summer of 1994) the Internet emerged as a central actor.

Summary

The book is organized into chapters that roughly alternate between legal and technological topics. My summary here just skims the surface.

The first two chapters introduce some of the characteristics and implications of electronic information technologies. We are in transition to that "mature electronic culture" people are starting to call cyberspace. The underlying technologies produce differences in how information is distributed, how we interact with it, its form (graphics and images as well as text), and its structure (hypertext vs. linear organization). Information technology does not just reduce time and improve efficiency; it compresses space and neutralizes distance. "Change occurs not only because time is less of a constraint but because space and distance are no longer obstacles to performing many informational tasks."

Information and its use are at the core of the legal process. Law and its evolution thus cannot be understood without taking into account how we communicate and work with information. When we change the information environment, we change the boundaries among informational things and the patterns of interaction among people. Technology is not neutral: it has obvious as well as unintended and unanticipated consequences for social arrangements. In law, one consequence of moving from print to pixels is a reduced sense of law as separate enterprise. Professional authority tends to decline when informational distances are smaller.

Chapter 3 looks at how the law library changes in an electronic incarnation. Visiting a "legal information place" whose materials are always "in" is different than interacting with a set of books in a print library. Such places need not obey Newtonian laws, nor observe any particular limits on the size of their collections. Distinctions between libraries, publishers, and online information providers cease being particularly useful. Legal information becomes available in abundance, to lawyers and nonprofessionals alike, but there are fewer certifying agents to vouch for the accuracy and authenticity of what is retrieved.

Chapter 4 examines three fundamental directions of movement in the changing information environment as we venture out from under the "umbrella of print": (1) toward information that is less stable and permanent, (2) away from mass production and distribution, and (3) toward machines that respond to and anticipate user actions. A change from movable type to "moving type" corresponds to the decline of the mass media. Unlike broadcast radio or television, or the printed book, electronic communication is inherently bidirectional—we give up information as we consume it, leaving behind a spreading electronic wake that poses new issues of privacy and consumer protection.

Contracts form the subject of chapter 5. Word processing, document assembly, and EDI (electronic data interchange) are changing how contracts are drafted and managed. This change in the medium of choice for information transactions—when paper becomes merely a transient copy of the "real," nonphysical document—may well be revolutionary. Electronic contracts become dynamic entities, potentially linking parties, monitoring compliance, and evolving to reflect changing circumstances. Text has become "electronified."

Chapter 6 discusses the ways in which electronic media enable greater use of visual communication. Machines that were thought limited to the manipulation of numbers and letters have turned out to be superb at processing images. Whereas print technology served to standardize, stabilize, and organize, visually rich electronic media may do the opposite.

Counsel Connect itself takes center stage in chapter 7, "Digital Lawyers: Working with Cyberspace." It serves as an example of how lawyers' modes of interaction and attitudes about information sharing can change in a new space. It also can be seen as an attempt to fortify deteriorating professional boundaries.

Chapter 8 deals with hypertext, providing plenty of opportunities to talk about seamless webs. Because it builds upon a different model for organizing knowledge, hypertext will exert pressure on the categories and boundaries in terms of which law and related affairs are conceived.

Assessment

A review is not complete without complaints. Katsh is not consistently successful in maintaining an unbroken narrative thread. A number of sections and paragraphs felt to me like they were written in other contexts and stitched in place because they had to go *somewhere*. Chapter 9, for instance, begins with truly beautiful passages about light, its rich metaphors, and its relationships to cyberspace. But the chapter then launches into discussions of copyright and privacy, excellent in themselves, that are only superficially linked to these ideas. And in a few parts the text reads like a tour through a clippings file, where one person after another is quoted or paraphrased: "As So-and-So has perceptively observed . . .; in the words of Somebody-Else . . . ."

But I enjoyed this book. It's a learned work, full of insights, information, and ideas that all of us can benefit from. It manages to be technically sophisticated without being obscure and avoids both utopian and dystopian temptations in painting law's fate at the hands of technology. There are extensive notes, a thorough bibliography, and a decent index.

Some will resist the conclusion that deep change is afoot. All this technology stuff, some say, will not fundamentally change what we do as lawyers and how we earn a living. I sympathize with the skeptics but think that events will prove them wrong. Many of Ethan Katsh's projections may turn out to be amusingly inaccurate with the benefit of a generation's hindsight, but the overall postulate of serious transformation seems dead-on right to me.

Let me close with a favorite quote (from page 194):

> The next generation of lawyers cannot rely on the exclusionary power
> of state-imposed and print-imposed boundaries to maintain the status,
> power, and distinction enjoyed by the profession in the past. If lawyers
> are to survive better than scribes or calligraphers did in the post-Guten-
> berg world, they need to do more than merely adapt new technologies
> to traditional practices and processes. The route to success lies in a new
> model of legal practice, in a new orientation toward and appreciation of
> electronic information, and in an understanding of the implications of
> shrinking distances between people and institutions.

Transforming the Law: Essays on Technology, Justice and the Legal Marketplace

By Richard Susskind
New York: Oxford University Press, 2000
ISBN 0-19-829922-2
292 pages

[A version of this review appeared in *Artificial Intelligence and Law* 9 (2001): 295–303]

Introduction

As the author puts it in the opening sentence, "This book is something of
a mixed bag." Only the first two chapters—Part I—are genuinely new,
covering just seventy-six pages, and they are the main focus of this
review. Part II contains four chapters drawn from or related to Susskind's
earlier book, *The Future of Law* (1996). Part III reaches even further back
and republishes four pieces from his work on legal expert systems in the
1980s. And Part IV, dedicated to the broader role of IT in the justice system, also contains revisions of essays written for other occasions.

It's useful to have these writings compiled in an updated and easily accessible collection. And the presence in one place of Susskind's broad-rang-
ing explorations of technical possibilities, philosophical underpinnings,
and business realities is a valuable testament to the rich multidisciplinar-
ity needed in approaching any of these subjects. But to my mind the primary value of this book is its introduction of a framework of ideas that
clarify the commercial and civic relevance—indeed the strategic central-
ity—of new "knowledge technologies."

Transforming the Law is an elegantly written book. It has a clear, engaging, pleasant style. It's full of interesting information and ideas. Some points may be old and some may be obvious, but they are organized in a vibrant, coherent whole. Contrary to many reading experiences these days—especially in technology contexts—it is free of typos and glaring word usage errors. Oxford University Press has admirably high production standards. (The only apparent error I noticed was the misplacement of material in Figure 1.11.)

Three themes undergird this book: (1) that the Internet and other information technologies will "fundamentally, irreversibly, and comprehensively change legal practice, the administration of justice, and the way in which non-lawyers handle their legal and quasi-legal affairs;" (2) that through those technologies people "will be able to identify and understand their legal rights and duties far more easily than has ever been possible in the past" and access "speedier, cheaper, and less combative mechanisms for resolving disputes;" and (3) that IT can and will increasingly be used to "capture, preserve, and disseminate legal knowledge and expertise" in support of such better access.

Richard Susskind is one of very few voices recognized internationally on the subject of IT-oriented reconceptualization of legal services. Few authors of comparable stature have given book-length treatment of these ideas. Ethan Katsh has written two books of equivalent scope (1989 and 1995), which are more scholarly and intellectually adventurous but less fitted for mainstream legal and business professionals. David Maister (1997) articulates many similar insights about the strategic importance of knowledge systems in professional services organizations but is less conversant with specific technologies or peculiarities of the legal domain. Others have championed similar ideas in short articles. See, e.g., Granat (1997), Hokkanen (1999), and Lauritsen (1990 and 2001).

Let's look more specifically at chapters 1 and 2, each of which revolves around a unifying model.

The Grid

I once heard a reasonably famous business speaker say, "It's the job of us consultants to simplify the world into two-by-two matrices." Susskind has found such a matrix, and it's a fertile one.

The basic idea is to plot a vertical internal-external axis against a horizontal technology-information-knowledge axis. The resulting quadrants then define four general categories into which law-related IT applications might fall. Here's a rough reconstruction.

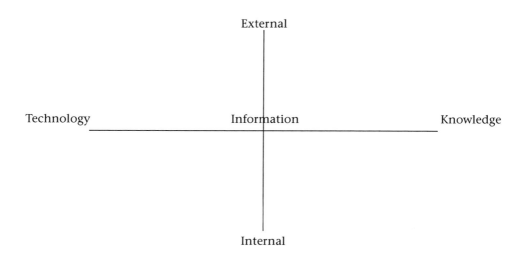

The up/down dimension is clear enough. Things on the upper part of the grid relate to a firm's external activities, its relations with clients (and presumably other outside actors, like suppliers, partners, and the public) Things on the bottom part are internal to the firm.

The left/right dimension represents a spectrum of processing sophistication, from "bare" technology handling simple data, through more generic information processing, and on into manipulation of advanced knowledge representations.

In the bottom left quadrant would be found the basic hardware, software, and networking infrastructures, along with such applications as time-keeping and accounting systems, document management, and litigation support—namely, those "back office" technologies supportive of law office operations but not generally visible to clients or the public and also not particularly high in programmed knowledge content. These are the foundational technologies no firm can afford to neglect.

Bottom-right technologies include many described today under the rubric of "knowledge management," such as know-how databases, precedent repositories, intelligent checklists, document assembly, and expert systems. These might be deployed on an intranet. Knowledge content is high, but these systems are still internally oriented, largely used by attorneys and other professionals within the virtual walls of the practice organization. Bottom-right systems promote internal efficiency and leverage human and other knowledge resources.

The top left quarter contains outwardly focused, operations-oriented applications, like e-mail links with clients, "deal rooms," and client-accessible matter-management systems. Some law firm extranets have this character. You can think of these technologies as better ways of doing traditional legal services.

The top right, finally, maps technologies that are high in both outward orientation and knowledge content. These include online advice systems, self-help document-assembly solutions, compliance audits, and computer-based training for clients. You can think of this area as the intersection of electronic commerce and knowledge management. Needless to say, this is where many of us with experiences both in legal AI and dot-com entrepreneurship feel the action is. This is the world of online legal services, "virtual lawyers," sexy new business opportunities, and radically new models for service delivery.

I suspect that most readers just being exposed to this framework will find it conceptually unsatisfying, especially in the crude form I've provided. There are a few immediate concerns. Technology, for instance, is pervasive in all four quadrants, so it seems a bit odd to have it labeled as the end of one of the axes. And the left/right distinction is somewhat ambiguous. In Susskind's discussion of the top half of the grid, it seems to signify the distinction between traditional or conventional legal services and new, innovative approaches. On the bottom half, the left/right distinction variously stands for back office vs. front office, foundation vs. superstructure, lesser vs. greater sophistication, and generic vs. domain-specific applications. These are all to be sure related, but they represent modes of differentiation whose nuances are lost when mixed.

It occurs to me that one characterization of the left/right dimension not explicitly discussed or rejected by Susskind would be that of *conduit* vs. *content*. The far left side represents pure "plumbing," with little regard to what is flowing in the pipes, and the far right represents the knowledge "stuff" that both lawyers and clients need, caring little about just how it is bottled and transported.

Susskind graciously acknowledges and addresses some of the shortcomings of his grid and makes a convincing case that its simplifications achieve the pragmatic purpose of providing a tool with which lawyers, technologists, and business analysts can communicate important ideas. Not only does it offer an easily understood framework onto which various technologies and initiatives can be meaningfully organized, but it serves as a theater within which major business strategy scenarios for a legal services provider can be rehearsed.

The second half of Chapter 1 uses the grid to explore and compare eight specific strategic alternatives in terms of which one or more quadrants are emphasized. For instance, "putting the house in order" is a strategic scenario of a firm that limits attention to the bottom two quadrants and rejects electronic commerce, at least for the short term.

Just as "above the fold" is where a day's most important stories appear on the front page of a newspaper, "above the line" is where law firms are advised to pay special attention. Yet, Susskind estimates that contemporary law firm IT budgets allocate a mere five percent to that territory. Similarly, most of the below-the-line activity is on the left, in the back-office, infrastructural arena. But Susskind also reports dramatic progress outward from the bottom left to the other quadrants between 1995 and 1999, at least among major law firms.

Not surprisingly, the only strategy Susskind enthusiastically endorses for a law firm "that wishes to enjoy commercial success in the new economy" is one of full commitment to all four corners of the grid ("law firms should be fully committed across all four quadrants by 2005") (p. 39). Top-notch back-office and client relationship systems will be expected as a matter of course, good internal knowledge management will increasingly be required, and competitive advantage will mainly be achieved by aggressive activity in the top right. It is also here that the transformation referenced in the book's title occurs.

The legal grid is interestingly reminiscent of a more famous 2 x 2 matrix, the one laid out in Stephen Covey's *The Seven Habits of Highly Effective People*, which plots the dimensions of important/not important and urgent/not urgent against each other. It turns out that the top right quarter of Covey's grid ("Quadrant 2") is especially notable as well, for it signifies things that are important but not urgent and that thus tend to be postponed and neglected. That well describes the state of Web services and other Susskind–Quadrant 2 initiatives at most law firms today. You might say that they are experiencing gridlock. But the critical mass of firms in London, New York, Sydney, and elsewhere that are now taking the online services challenge seriously—not to mention global accounting/consulting firms and other nimble new competitors—will heighten the urgency of such activity across the profession.

One last overlay of the grid that confirms its versatility is that of human resources—namely, what kinds of people are needed to lead work across different swaths of the legal technology landscape? Susskind persuasively allocates the roles of chief technology officer, chief information officer, and chief knowledge officer to three vertical slices of the grid, ordered left to right, respectively. Few firms will in fact have a CTO, a CIO, *and* a CKO, but most will need to understand those positions as distinct roles that call upon different skill sets and respond to different aspects of their overall strategy.

The Chain

Chapter 2 introduces a second model for thinking about how information technology will catalyze transformations in the legal system—that of the "client service chain." This is basically a view of the legal services process as comprising three phases: *recognition, selection,* and *service.* Today's service chain typically consists of (1) a "blatant trigger"—an event or circumstance that unambiguously calls for legal attention, causing a person to recognize the need for professional help; (2) selection of a lawyer through a variety of conventional channels (prior familiarity, family relation or friendship, local presence, advertising, reputation, etc.); and (3) service delivery in the form of traditional one-to-one counsel, guidance, and matter management.

The paradigm today is one of reactive, not proactive, measures. It encapsulates a lawyer-centric, case-by-case, face-to-face model of how people get their legal needs met. But each aspect of the contemporary service chain is open to creative deconstruction at the hands of new technologies and business models. Classical intermediaries like lawyers are particularly vulnerable to disintermediation and reintermediation.

In the *recognition* part of the chain, today's blatant-trigger, reactive model is likely to be displaced, or at least complemented, by proactive facilities that draw upon IT to give early warnings and help prevent legal mishaps. These include legal audits, push technologies (automatically alerting people based on their stored profiles, rather than requiring them to seek and "pull" relevant information), intelligent agents (which can serve both to recognize problems and suggest solutions), and arrangements that embed legal expertise right within clients' operational business systems. Susskind's vivid point on this front is that "clients would like a fence at the top of the cliff rather than an ambulance at the bottom" (p. 262).

In the *selection* phase, today's confusing, choice-limited, information-poor processes for finding an appropriate service provider are being supplemented with online auctions, new "infomediaries" that match clients and lawyers, and virtual teams of professionals who assemble dynamically in response to particular configurations of need. The selection step will also increasingly result in the purchase of "unbundled" services, where tasks are allocated among the client, information systems, and zero or more lawyers as needed and desired.

In the *service*-delivery (or, perhaps better understood, service-*receiving*) stage, today's conventional direct-consultation lawyering model will give way to multi-provider, unbundled, machine-based, and other creative ways to address the underlying legal need. Online legal services in particular will commoditize many routine services, providing increased consumer choice, lower prices, and perhaps even higher quality. This may not bode well for lawyers not adept at change. But as Susskind notes, "the law and legal institutions are no more there to provide a livelihood for lawyers than ill-health exists to provide a living for doctors" (p. 49).

The linear service chain of today effectively becomes a web of routes through which people discover and deal with their legal needs.

Just like his grid, Susskind's client service chain is open to various forms of conceptual challenge. Elsewhere in contemporary business literature, "service chain" is often used in analogy to "supply chain" or "demand chain"—that is, as sequences of steps in which different participants add value in a process. A richer model of the legal service chain would encompass contributions to the legal value package from law schools ("suppliers" of lawyers), law publishers, and legal software and other tool providers. But again, the admitted simplifications of this model yield a valuable prism through which to explore important policies and opportunities.

The latter part of Chapter 2 includes discussion of the "disruptive technologies" concept popularized by Clayton Christensen in *The Innovator's Dilemma* (1997). Susskind gives a compelling portrayal of the deep conflict many law firms will find themselves in as they try to balance resources between technologies that sustain their current, profitable business models and disruptive ones like online legal services that appear to threaten those models but which may turn out to be essential for long-term survival. This dilemma will be sharpened by the huge accounting and consulting firms, which have begun to attack aggressively the legal marketplace and which are not burdened with cultural and structural commitments to traditional legal service models. The chapter appropriately concludes with six broad strategies for legal businesses to follow, such as establishing an off-site "new economy unit" and setting up online resources for every matter that serve the differing needs of the client, the in-house team, the other parties, and perhaps even the public.

Legal Futures

Part II of this book represents many of the provocative ideas first put forth in Susskind's 1996 *The Future of Law*. Those who haven't read that book, or its 1998 revised edition in paperback, will find the four chapters here a handy alternative. They lay out a comprehensive vision of how today's "legal paradigm" of service and process will morph into tomorrow's. For instance, we will move from advisory, one-to-one services to informational, one-to-many services. We will migrate from legal problem solving to legal risk management, from dispute resolution to dispute preemption, from a dedicated, single legal profession to largely distinct callings of advocate/advisors and legal knowledge engineers.

Another important theme from this earlier work is the "latent legal market"—that broad world of situations in the everyday lives of people and businesses that would benefit from legal guidance but have not so benefited because available services are too expensive, cumbersome, time-consuming, or otherwise forbidding. The availability of simple, cheap online legal services could liberate a lot of this kind of demand.

Again, Susskind does a good job of weaving available (or imaginable) technologies into these business contexts and opportunities, and his analyses hold up quite well against the intervening years. Chapter 5, "The Likely and the Possible," drawn from the 1998 paperback edition, and Chapter 6, "A Response to Critics," from 1999 provide a nice bridge between the 1996 book and the newest parts of the current one. I'm particularly gratified that Susskind stops frequently to emphasize the untenable inadequacy of legal services in modern societies for the poor and disadvantaged and the ways in which that problem can begin to be addressed by the technical and business innovations chronicled here.

Taking Action

Those of us who have gone to battle in the right-side quadrants know the stunning difficulty of sophisticated legal knowledge engineering and of exploiting these ideas commercially. Can we live up to the visions Susskind lays out for the legal world?

If you are an AI and law type and haven't already read this book, you should. For a cogent admixture of insightful business analysis and technology reporting, this is about as good as it gets. People dedicated to understanding the challenges and potentials of knowledge engineering in the world of law should appreciate the business ideas and realities that structure that world.

If you're a lawyer or law firm administrator, the first several chapters are just about essential reading. Even if you ultimately reject some of the ideas contained there, you need to understand them. Your best competition does.

References

Granat, Richard, S., From Legal Services to Information Services. *Internet Practice Newsletter*, May 1997. [Available at **http://www.granat.com/ legalservice.html**.]

Hokkanen, John, Investing in Technology: A Business Framework. *Managing Partner*, Vol. 2, No. 4, 8–13, 1999. [Available at **http://www.llrx.com/ features/investing.htm**.]

Katsh, M. Ethan, *The Electronic Media and the Transformation of Law*. New York: Oxford University Press, 1989.

Katsh, M. Ethan *Law in a Digital World*, New York: Oxford University Press, 1995.

Lauritsen, M., Delivering Legal Services with Computer-based Practice Systems *Clearinghouse Review*. Vol. 23, 1532–1539, April 1990.

Lauritsen, M., Lawyering for Tomorrow: Technology and the Future of International Law Practice. In J. Drolshammer and M. Pfeifer (Eds.), *The Internationalization of the Practice of Law*, The Hague: Kluwer Law International, 411–421, 2001.

Maister, David H., *Managing the Professional Service Firm*. New York: Simon & Schuster, 1997.

Common Sense: On the Information Revolution and Your Job

Murdock, John E. and Terry L. Crum, *Common Sense: On the Information Revolution and Your Job,* Colombo, Sri Lanka: Lake House Printers and Publishers, PLC, 2002.
$19.95. ISBN 0-9723020-0-X

[This originally appeared in *Law Practice*, March 2004, p. 62]

"This book is about information, not technology. It is the place where business managers and technology specialists find common ground."

That statement on its back cover pretty much captures the message and flavor of this thoughtful, plain-spoken book. John Murdock, partner in a

Nashville law firm, and Terry Crum, chief knowledge officer in a Cleveland firm, have collaborated over the past decade to explore the common ground referred to above. They've now done a great job in laying out their insights for the rest of us.

Regular readers of *Law Practice* and similar periodicals covering the intersections of business, management, and technology have probably developed, as I have, a knee-jerk cynicism about purportedly fresh explanations of "how the information revolution will change what you do for a living." How many times do we need to be told, for instance, that business goals need to drive technical solutions, not vice versa? That "what to do" should take precedence over "how to do"?

Well, the right answer probably is "As many times as it takes." Lots of our organizations have yet to learn even that simple lesson. Persuasive writing that nails home points like that should be welcome.

Refreshingly free of jargon, and punctuated by down-to-earth anecdotes, analogies, quotes, and illustrations, *Common Sense* will be especially useful for getting such points across to nontechnical professionals who are averse to glossy materials and breathless pronouncements. They may arrive at powerful new insights about information and its management. But even jaded legal techies and others who think they already "get it" will discover new perspectives on critical issues.

Don't come at this book expecting academic rigor. The authors make lots of blanket statements one instinctively thinks of exceptions to. Some of their analytical frameworks don't quite balance. I find their sharp distinction between *productivity* and *effectiveness* a bit forced, for instance. It is, of course, useful to recognize that internal cost savings brought about by new technologies may not yield better service to customers, but at least for me that pair of words does not readily capture that difference.

An arguably oversimplified field of three information *containers* (brains, paper, digital media) and four information *functions* (store, retrieve, move, process) turns out to yield a nice harvest of observations. And that prepares the way for a wise set of recommended principles, like "Information Should Be Given All Possible Context."

Most of *Common Sense* discusses these issues in terms applicable to any business context, but Chapter 4—styled a "case study"—focuses on law offices. You will enjoy reading about "lawyers who dwell in caves," "lawyers who farm," and "lawyers who fly." Our challenge is to both fly and remain grounded.

Knowledge Management and the Smarter Lawyer

By Gretta Rusanow
ALM Publishing: New York, 2003
500 pages

[This originally appeared in *Legal Management*, March/April 2004]

It's hard to talk about knowledge management (KM) for very long without starting to sound clichéd and jargonish. (I've tried—and failed—more than a few times.) Gretta Rusanow does better than most in her recent book, *Knowledge Management and the Smarter Lawyer*. In fact, she does quite well. This is a very timely and useful book.

The book consists of thirteen chapters, organized into four parts.

- Part I—"Knowledge Management and the Business of Law"—introduces the basic concepts and business motivations behind KM.
- Part II—"Critical Elements of Knowledge Management"—lays out the wide scope of KM initiatives, the organizational options for their pursuit, the cultural challenges, and the relevant technologies.
- Part III—"How to Approach Knowledge Management"—gets into strategy and implementation details, as well as value metrics and new dynamics of client service.
- Part IV—"Knowledge Management for Other Shapes and Sizes"—covers themes more specific to law departments and solo practitioners. (Most of the earlier material is medium- and large-firm oriented.)

The chapters contain many specific examples ("case studies" that seem based on real situations but mention no names) and detailed checklists. Along the way readers will find a wealth of handy frameworks, job descriptions, and practical guidance. There's a helpful glossary and a decent index.

Rusanow—an Australian lawyer with a consulting practice based in Sydney and New York—has delivered a carefully written and thorough treatment of most important KM issues. She takes an admirably broad view about the kinds of knowledge, the kinds of approaches, and the kinds of people involved in the process. Not just the practice of law, but the business of law. Not just repositories of precedents and best practices, but mentoring and debriefing. Not just lawyers, but paralegals, secretaries, and administrative staff.

The author also stresses the ongoingness of KM efforts: "Knowledge management is not a project with a completion date. This is about adopting new ways to work that, over time, become deeply engrained in the work processes within your firm" (p. 51).

Those who read this book straight through will encounter considerable repetition and wish for more stylistic variation. Besides *knowledge* and *management*, the word *initiative* must occur a thousand times. There are so many "critical" and "key" points it's hard to know which are most important. And many lawyers I know cringe at the thought of having their know-how "captured."

I also found myself writing "duh" in the margins a couple times. ("The amount of money you have to spend on knowledge management will determine the scope of your implementation efforts" (p. 327). "It is unlikely that KM is the sole initiative of your law firm" (p. 332). But seeming platitudes can remind us of important truths.

Some legal KM pundits commit the sin of overemphasizing technology. Rusanow errs on the opposite side. It is clearly important to give primary stress to the human and cultural dimensions. But she envisions—in my opinion—an overly anemic role for technology, relegated largely to providing a passive conduit for humanly expressed knowledge. There is little attention to "smart" software, or machine intelligence. To my mind, that is to throw the (robotic?) baby out with the bath water. Expert systems, dynamic documents, intelligent checklists, and other tools increasingly house and exercise knowledge in law offices—knowledge that needs to be managed. Advanced nonbiological knowledge systems could well turn out to be central to law in the twenty-first century.

Here are other complaints:

- ♦ You wouldn't know by reading this book that there is an already substantial literature on its topics and that a large international community of scholars, consultants, and vendors actively work in the area. It's more than a little ironic not to reference some of the knowledge that has been codified about legal KM itself. Only a couple works are mentioned in footnotes. A bibliography should be considered for the next edition, referencing works by Adam Bendell, Neil Cameron, Ron Friedmann, Richard Granat, John Hokkanen, Dennis Kennedy, Peter Krakaur, Kingsley Martin, Nina Platt, LaVern Pritchard, Alan Rothman, and Richard Susskind, to mention just a few.

- I have yet to come across a truly satisfying distinction between "mere information" and "knowledge." People use the terms too many different ways in too many different contexts. Rusanow's formulation—"Knowledge is value added by people" or "human effort applied to information" (p. 69)—implies that there is a well-settled difference. The difference between explicit and tacit knowledge also seems oversimplified, at least as applied to examples.

- Although I agree that hourly billing is one major obstacle to KM success, I don't think it is accurate to say, "Where a law firm bases it compensation levels purely on the number of billable hours, there is *no* room for knowledge management" (p. 135; emphasis added here and in following quotes), "If law firms continue to bill by the hour, there is simply no incentive to reduce the time spent on specific tasks" (p. 194), or that "It leaves *no* room for investment in the future growth of the firm" (p. 195). What about basic professionalism, decency, or competition? Haven't they sometimes motivated even hard-core time billers to work efficiently and to share knowledge? And hourly-billing-free sanctuaries like law departments and nonprofit legal services operations have hardly found KM unchallenging.

- This nonchalant absolutism surfaces in a couple other places. "Without the contribution of *all* staff to knowledge management, your firm will *fail* in its knowledge management efforts" (p. 204). "The *only* way your firm can really capture, share, and leverage its knowledge across all offices is to have a standard technology platform" (p. 252). "The *only* product of a law firm is its knowledge" (p. 276). (Knowledge per se is admittedly sometimes a product, but much more often it is only the raw material for or catalyst of the real product most clients pay for—namely, an accomplished legal *result.* I think this is more than semantics.)

I sometimes doubt that knowledge management is a discrete discipline, rather than the fertile intersection of *people* management, *information* science, and knowledge *technology*. Books like this ease my doubt. Despite the above quibbles, I find *Knowledge Management and the Smarter Lawyer* a very valuable contribution to the literature. It is thought provoking and mind expanding. At almost five hundred pages, it is hardly a quick read. But it is well worth the effort. Nearly anyone who works in or with a law office will benefit by coming to terms with its ideas.

Index

Companion Web site

Supplemental and updated materials are available at **www.SmarterLegal Work.com**

Selected Books from . . .
THE ABA LAW PRACTICE MANAGEMENT SECTION

The Lawyer's Guide to Collaboration Tools and Technologies: Smart Ways to Work Together
By Dennis Kennedy and Tom Mighell
This first-of-its-kind guide for the legal profession shows you how to use standard technology you already have and the latest "Web 2.0" resources and other tech tools, like Google Docs, Microsoft Office and Share-Point, and Adobe Acrobat, to work more effectively on projects with colleagues, clients, co-counsel and even opposing counsel. In *The Lawyer's Guide to Collaboration Tools and Technologies: Smart Ways to Work Together*, well-known legal technology authorities Dennis Kennedy and Tom Mighell provides a wealth of information useful to lawyers who are just beginning to try these tools, as well as tips and techniques for those lawyers with intermediate and advanced collaboration experience.

The Lawyer's Guide to Marketing on the Internet, Third Edition
By Gregory H. Siskind, Deborah McMurray, and Richard P. Klau
In today's competitive environment, it is critical to have a comprehensive online marketing strategy that uses all the tools possible to differentiate your firm and gain new clients. The Lawyer's Guide to Marketing on the Internet, in a completely updated and revised third edition, showcases practical online strategies and the latest innovations so that you can immediately participate in decisions about your firm's Web marketing effort. With advice that can be implemented by established and young practices alike, this comprehensive guide will be a crucial component to streamlining your marketing efforts.

The Lawyer's Guide to Adobe Acrobat, Third Edition
By David L. Masters
This book was written to help lawyers increase productivity, decrease costs, and improve client services by moving from paper-based files to digital records. This updated and revised edition focuses on the ways lawyers can benefit from using the most current software, Adobe® Acrobat 8, to create Portable Document Format (PDF) files.

PDF files are reliable, easy-to-use, electronic files for sharing, reviewing, filing, and archiving documents across diverse applications, business processes, and platforms. The format is so reliable that the federal courts' Case Management/Electronic Case Files (CM/ECF) program and state courts that use Lexis-Nexis File & Serve have settled on PDF as the standard.

You'll learn how to:

- Create PDF files from a number of programs, including Microsoft Office
- Use PDF files the smart way
- Markup text and add comments
- Digitally, and securely, sign documents
- Extract content from PDF files
- Create electronic briefs and forms

The Electronic Evidence and Discovery Handbook: Forms, Checklists, and Guidelines
By Sharon D. Nelson, Bruce A. Olson, and John W. Simek
The use of electronic evidence has increased dramatically over the past few years, but many lawyers still struggle with the complexities of electronic discovery. This substantial book provides lawyers with the templates they need to frame their discovery requests and provides helpful advice on what they can subpoena. In addition to the ready-made forms, the authors also supply explanations to bring you up to speed on the electronic discovery field. The accompanying CD-ROM features over 70 forms, including, Motions for Protective Orders, Preservation and Spoliation Documents, Motions to Compel, Electronic Evidence Protocol Agreements, Requests for Production, Internet Services Agreements, and more. Also included is a full electronic evidence case digest with over 300 cases detailed!

The 2010 Solo and Small Firm Legal Technology Guide
By Sharon D. Nelson, Esq., John W. Simek, and Michael C. Maschke
This annual guide is the only one of its kind written to help solo and small firm lawyers find the best technology for their dollar. You'll find the most current information and recommendations on computers, servers, networking equipment, legal software, printers, security products, smart phones, and anything else a law office might need. It's written in clear, easily understandable language to make implementation easier if you choose to do it yourself, or you can use it in conjunction with your IT consultant. Either way, you'll learn how to make technology work for you.

The Law Firm Associate's Guide to Personal Marketing and Selling Skills
By Catherine Alman MacDonagh and Beth Marie Cuzzone
This is the first volume in ABA's new groundbreaking Law Firm Associates Development Series, created to teach important skills that associates and other lawyers need to succeed at their firms, but that they may have not learned in law school. This volume focuses on personal marketing and sales skills. It covers creating a personal marketing plan, finding people within your target market, preparing for client meetings, "asking" for business, realizing marketing opportunities, keeping your clients, staying in touch with your network inside and outside the firm, and more. An accompanying trainer's manual illustrating how to best structure the sessions and use the book is available to firms to facilitate group training sessions.

Many law firms expect their new associates to hit the ground running when they are hired on. Although firms often take the time to bring these associates up to speed on client matters, they can be reluctant to invest the time needed to train them how to improve personal skills such as marketing. This book will serve as a brief, easy-to-digest primer for associates on how to develop and use marketing and selling techniques.

The Lawyer's Guide to Concordance
By Liz M. Weiman

In this age, when trial outcomes depend on the organization of electronic data discovery, *The Lawyer's Guide to Concordance* reveals how attorneys and staff can make Concordance the most powerful tool in their litigation arsenal. Using this easy-to-read hands-on reference guide, individuals who are new to Concordance can get up-to-speed quickly, by following its step-by-step instructions, exercises, and time-saving shortcuts. For those already working with Concordance, this comprehensive resource provides methods, strategies, and technical information to further their knowledge and success using this robust program.

Inside The Lawyer's Guide to Concordance readers will also find:

- Techniques to effectively search database records, create tags for the results, customize printed reports, redline and redact images, create production sets
- Strategies to create and work with transcript, e-document, and e-mail databases, load files from vendors, manage images, troubleshoot, and more
- Real-world case studies from law firms in the United States and England describing Concordance features that have improved case management

The Lawyer's Guide to CT Summation iBlaze, Second Edition
By Tom O'Connor

CT Summation iBlaze gives you complete control over litigation evidence by bringing all you need—transcripts, documents, issues, and events, to your fingertips in one easy-to-use software program. Working in close collaboration with CT Summation, author and noted technology speaker Tom O'Connor has developed this easy-to-understand guide designed to quickly get you up and running on CT Summation software. Fully up-to-date, covering the latest version of iBlaze, the book features step-by-step instructions on the functions of iBlaze and how to get the most from this powerful, yet easy-to-use program.

The Lawyer's Guide to Microsoft Word 2007
By Ben M. Schorr

Microsoft Word is one of the most used applications in the Microsoft Office suite—there are few applications more fundamental than putting words on paper. Most lawyers use Word and few of them get everything they can from it. Because the documents you create are complex and important—your law practice depends, to some degree, upon the quality of the documents you produce and the efficiency with which you can produce them. Focusing on the tools and features that are essential for lawyers in their everyday practice, *The Lawyer's Guide to Microsoft Word* explains in detail the key components to help make you more effective, more efficient and more successful.

The Lawyer's Guide to Microsoft Excel 2007
By John C. Tredennick

Did you know Excel can help you analyze and present your cases more effectively or help you better understand and manage complex business transactions? Designed as a hands-on manual for beginners as well as longtime spreadsheet users, you'll learn how to build spreadsheets from scratch, use them to analyze issues, and to create graphics presentation. Key lessons include:

- Spreadsheets 101: How to get started for beginners
- Advanced Spreadsheets: How to use formulas to calculate values for settlement offers, and damages, business deals
- Simple Graphics and Charts: How to make sophisticated charts for the court or to impress your clients
- Sorting and filtering data and more

How to Start and Build a Law Practice, Platinum Fifth Edition
By Jay G. Foonberg

This classic ABA bestseller has been used by tens of thousands of lawyers as the comprehensive guide to planning, launching, and growing a successful practice. It's packed with over 600 pages of guidance on identifying the right location, finding clients, setting fees, managing your office, maintaining an ethical and responsible practice, maximizing available resources, upholding your standards, and much more. You'll find the information you need to successfully launch your practice, run it at maximum efficiency, and avoid potential pitfalls along the way. If you're committed to starting—and growing—your own practice, this one book will give you the expert advice you need to make it succeed for years to come.

The Lawyer's Guide to Microsoft Outlook 2007
By Ben M. Schorr

Outlook is the most used application in Microsoft Office, but are you using it to your greatest advantage? *The Lawyer's Guide to Microsoft Outlook 2007* is the only guide written specifically for lawyers to help you be more productive, more efficient and more successful. More than just email, Outlook is also a powerful task, contact, and scheduling manager that will improve your practice. From helping you log and track phone calls, meetings, and correspondence to archiving closed case material in one easy-to-store location, this book unlocks the secrets of "underappreciated" features that you will use every day. Written in plain language by a twenty-year veteran of law office technology and ABA member, you'll find:

- Tips and tricks to effectively transfer information between all components of the software
- The eight new features in Outlook 2007 that lawyers will love
- A tour of major product features and how lawyers can best use them
- Mistakes lawyers should avoid when using Outlook
- What to do when you're away from the office

30-Day Risk-Free Order Form
Call Today! 1-800-285-2221
Monday–Friday, 7:30 AM – 5:30 PM, Central Time

Qty	Title	LPM Price	Regular Price	Total
_____	The Lawyer's Guide to Collaboration Tools and Technologies: Smart Ways to Work Together (5110589)	$59.95	$ 89.95	$_____
_____	The Lawyer's Guide to Marketing on the Internet, Third Edition (5110585)	74.95	84.95	$_____
_____	The Lawyer's Guide to Adobe Acrobat, Third Edition (5110588)	49.95	79.95	$_____
_____	The Electronic Evidence and Discovery Handbook: Forms, Checklists, and Guidelines (5110569)	99.95	129.95	$_____
_____	The 2010 Solo and Small Firm Legal Technology Guide (5110701)	54.95	89.95	$_____
_____	The Law Firm Associate's Guide to Personal Marketing and Selling Skills (5110582)	39.95	49.95	$_____
_____	Trainer's Manual for the Law Firm Associate's Guide to Personal Marketing and Selling Skills (5110581)	49.95	59.95	$_____
_____	The Lawyer's Guide to Concordance (5110666)	49.95	69.95	$_____
_____	The Lawyer's Guide to CT Summation iBlaze, Second Edition (5110698)	49.95	69.95	$_____
_____	The Lawyer's Guide to Microsoft Word 2007 (5110697)	49.95	69.95	$_____
_____	The Lawyer's Guide to Microsoft Excel 2007 (5110665)	49.95	69.95	$_____
_____	How to Start and Build a Law Practice, Platinum Fifth Edition (5110508)	57.95	69.95	$_____
_____	The Lawyer's Guide to Microsoft Outlook 2007 (5110661)	49.99	69.99	$_____

*Postage and Handling	
$10.00 to $49.99	$5.95
$50.00 to $99.99	$7.95
$100.00 to $199.99	$9.95
$200.00+	$12.95

**Tax
DC residents add 5.75%
IL residents add 10.25%

*Postage and Handling	$_____
**Tax	$_____
TOTAL	$_____

PAYMENT

❏ Check enclosed (to the ABA)

❏ Visa   ❏ MasterCard   ❏ American Express

_____
Account Number   Exp. Date   Signature

Name _____ Firm _____
Address _____
City _____ State _____ Zip _____
Phone Number _____ E-Mail Address _____

Guarantee

If—for any reason—you are not satisfied with your purchase, you may return it within 30 days of receipt for a complete refund of the price of the book(s). No questions asked!

Mail: ABA Publication Orders, P.O. Box 10892, Chicago, Illinois 60610-0892
♦ Phone: 1-800-285-2221 ♦ FAX: 312-988-5568

E-Mail: abasvcctr@abanet.org ♦ Internet: http://www.lawpractice.org/catalog